Faith, Social Justice, and Public Policy:
A Progressive's View by Gary E. Maring

Schroeder Stribling, Director of N Street Village (serves homeless women in DC)

Gary Maring's voice is critically important for our times – this book is an exhortation to people of all spiritual traditions to respond in faith to the serious social justice issues of today. His perspective echoes the passionate response of the interfaith founders of N Street Village which has become a demonstration of hope and reconciliation on the small scale of our city. I trust that his words will inspire and encourage its readers to create and sustain other such effective examples of justice and social change.

Pastor Karen Brau, Luther Place Memorial Church in DC

At a time when there are very loud public voices around what it means to be Christian, Gary Maring offers up a wide offering of faithful and prophetic writings that broaden the Christian conversation. Gary makes authentic arguments for an engaged and progressive Christianity, offering us insights from his first hand experience with women who are struggling with homelessness and poverty. The book is well worth the read.

John Steinbruck, Former pastor of Luther Place

I served with Gary Maring nearly three decades. Gary is a spiritual person, transformed by his faith, but his is a spirituality that prioritizes the reality of this world. The poor, the oppressed, the marginal, are given energetic and passionate commitment and support in this writer's biblically informed focus and attention. Gary encounters the homeless and weak as embodying Jesus' suffering presence with us daily on our urban asphalt deserts... Justice in this world becomes Gary's "reason for being"__ this is as I read him in his life and newly inspired text.

Faith,
Social Justice,
and
Public Policy

———

A Progressive's View

Gary E. Maring

Contents

Preface

This is both an exciting and daunting time in human history to be living. Our species, the modern version of Homo sapiens, appeared about a hundred thousand years ago. It took about sixty thousand years to learn how to use tools, and it was only about ten thousand years ago that man began to settle into communities and begin early agricultural practices. Yet in only a hundred years, we have gone from horse-and-buggy transportation to space travel. Knowledge is increasing at an exponential rate. Just over 150 years ago, it took the pony express ten days to get a message across our country. Today, information technology connects us globally in real time. Our knowledge of the universe has expanded dramatically in the last few decades, aided by the Hubble telescope, which has allowed us to see light that originated from galaxies just over 13 billion years ago; amazingly, just 600 billion years after the Big Bang. Science now tells us that there are hundreds of billions of stars in our galaxy and hundreds of millions of other galaxies in the universe. Astronomers are increasingly discovering planets within our universe, some of which may have the necessary conditions for at least primitive forms of life. In this century, we will likely travel to neighboring planets or asteroids within our galaxy and possibly encounter life in some form beyond the earth.

Further, we are in the early stages of an information revolution at least as profound as the industrial revolution. The emerging social media provide for unprecedented interaction within communities, within nations, and globally. In some recent cases, these social media are being credited with national revolutions. Repressive regimes can no longer completely control the message within their societies. We are also in the early stages of a religious transformation (some say another reformation); many in society are moving beyond institutional churches and rigid doctrines to a more spiritual-oriented faith where consumers shop for spiritual communities that meet their needs. At the same time, there are those within each of the major religious traditions who seem threatened by these rapid changes in their religion and society and at times actively resist this change, sometimes in violent ways. Modernity, along with its inevitable scientific advancements, has always been a threat to some in the religious community as it is today with many in the Religious Right. Perhaps most disturbing is the fact that prominent politicians are pandering to the Religious Right with anti-science political rhetoric. Cornelius's scientific theory, later supported by Galileo, that the earth was not the center of the solar system, was very unsettling to the church hierarchy some five hundred years ago; but science and religion were both able to move beyond that crisis. Today, mainline religious denominations accept the important role of science in the advancement of our society and yet are able to appreciate the beauty and wisdom of ancient Biblical narratives such as Genesis.

While technology and the knowledge revolution provide great opportunities for society, unprecedented global challenges are also before us. The global population is estimated to have reached 7 billion in 2011; China and India alone have well over a billion people each. The world is growing at the rate of about a billion additional people every twelve years. The ability to feed, provide clean water, provide health services, and prevent massive violence or genocide within this global population is testing our limits now and will only get worse. With the growth in population and increased resource consumption and pollution, global environmental sustainability is at risk. The National Academy of Sciences report, *America's Climate Choices,*[1] finds that climate change poses significant risks to human society and the environment. Also, many of earth's species are disappearing at an alarming rate; polar bears are the most recent species under threat as a result of the arctic ice melting earlier and earlier each year.

Global violence continues to be a major concern. Increasing access to weapons of violence by those who are actively resisting postmodern trends in society and religion has resulted in dramatic terrorist events such as 9/11. Weapons of mass destruction threaten man's existence as we know it. Mass violence and genocides continue to devastate societies around the world, even though we said "never again" after the Holocaust.

These issues are no longer confined to small parts of the world. The United States inevitably gets drawn into these challenges, both nationally and internationally. How will our national and global institutions respond to these unprecedented changes and challenges? What role will our nation's faith communities play, both domestically and globally, in these challenging public policy issues? That latter question is largely the subject of this book; that is, the role of faith and justice in public policy.

I have to admit to a few biases before starting. First, I am both progressive and faith-oriented. Second, although I grew up as a Christian and am currently an active member of the Memorial Evangelical Lutheran Church (hereafter referred to as Luther Place) in Washington, DC, I feel strongly that Christians do not have the exclusive path to God. The idea summarized by Archbishop Desmond Tutu of South Africa in the title of his new book, *God Is Not a Christian* resonates with me. Third, I am a strong believer in faith-based social justice as preached by Jesus and the great prophets of the Old Testament or Hebrew Bible. I come from a background of forty years of helping develop social justice ministries through Luther Place church. I came to live and work in Washington DC in 1967, and I soon saw the nation rocked by the assassinations of Martin Luther King Jr. (MLK) and Bobby Kennedy in the spring of 1968. Following MLK's assassination, riots broke out in DC near our church on Thomas Circle, and the Fourteenth Street corridor went up in flames. The church was a place of refuge during that period, and this was to be a turning point in the life and mission of the church. Out of that tragedy, the congregation regrouped, and in the process called an activist urban pastor, John Steinbruck, from Easton, Pennsylvania, to help us find a new mission. This was in 1970. Pastor John gradually helped open our eyes to the social justice message of the gospels, and he guided us in how to be good stewards of our church property and resources. N Street Village, a continuum of services for homeless and formerly homeless women, grew out of some old, run-down townhouses and a parking lot owned by the church. Support for N Street Village came from people of many faiths, so this experience significantly impacts my belief in interfaith dialogue, cooperation, and respect for each other's religious traditions. N Street supporters from the multiple faiths resonated with the underpinning biblical texts inscribed on the entrance to N Street Village (see photo below) as follows:

- "I was a stranger and you welcomed me…anything you did for the humblest, you did for me." (Matthew 25:35, 40)
- "The stranger who sojourns with you shall be to you as the native among you, and you shall love the stranger as yourself." (Leviticus 19:34)
- "Do not neglect to show hospitality to the stranger; for thereby some have entertained angels unawares." (Hebrews 13:2)

**N Street Village courtyard entrance
with Matthew 25 biblical inscription displayed**

Today, nearly forty years after its founding by Luther Place, N Street Village is a wonderful testament to what a church, in collaboration with other faith communities, government, and the private sector, can do with its resources to help achieve justice in our society. N Street Village now serves more than 60 percent of the population of homeless women in DC. I would invite all who read this book to come tour N Street Village to see it firsthand and learn more about homelessness and comprehensive approaches to solving it.

I firmly believe that the progressive faith and spiritual communities, along with secular advocates of social justice, can work together to play significant roles in promoting justice in their local communities and in our nation. There is a critical national debate taking place at this moment in history about what direction our country will take, including the role of government in helping assure justice in society. Thus I felt compelled to write this book promoting collaborative action toward social justice in our communities and the nation's public policies.

I indicate in the title of my book that it is written from a Progressive's viewpoint; what do I mean by that? In regard to my religious tradition, it means a strong social justice orientation as advocated by the great biblical prophets, including Jesus. In a progressive religious tradition, critical analysis and debate of the meaning of biblical texts in both their historical setting and in our modern society is encouraged. This allows us to understand, for example, that just because women were subjugated in ancient societies of the Bible doesn't mean that it is appropriate to replicate that in contemporary society. We understand that both the Old Testament (Hebrew Bible) and the New Testament texts only emerged after a significant time of oral tradition. The Old Testament oral tradition went on for several centuries before the stories were written down by the various authors. In the case of the New Testament Gospels, there was at least a forty- to seventy-year oral tradition until the Gospels were completed by the four authors who most scholars agree never met Jesus, so it is perfectly understandable that there are many conflicts among their accounts of Jesus and his ministry. This understanding does not diminish the richness of the stories, parables, and lessons to be learned from the Old and New Testament texts for current and succeeding generations of Jews and Christians. Finally, on the issue of salvation, I am with major theologians like N. T. Wright and Marcus Borg, reviewed herein. They suggest that the biblical focus of salvation is much more about restoring wholeness to all in this world (heaven on earth) than on some hereafter where only the select few are redeemed (and as prominent Evangelical pastor Rob Bell asks about the latter view, are we to presume that the remaining billions and billions of people who aren't "saved" are to burn in hell forever?).[2] At Luther Place, our focus is on restoration of the Kingdom of God, that is, peace and justice, here and now for all of God's people, including the homeless we host at Luther Place and N Street Village.

Historically, in the U.S. Progressive context, I would have had much in common with the human rights initiatives of the Social Gospel movement in the early part of the twentieth century and the Catholic Worker Movement led by Dorothy Day, which promoted social justice policies during the Depression. Politically, these religious movement positions largely aligned with progressive policies advanced by Presidents Theodore Roosevelt and Franklin Delano Roosevelt (FDR), respectively. These combined religious and political progressive movements were to result in major social justice accomplishments in the first half of the twentieth century such as women's suffrage, government reform and civil service, workplace regulations (e.g., child labor laws), fair wages, social security and unemployment measures, industrial reform and regulation (e.g. Teddy Roosevelt taking on the "robber barons" of his day), environmental conservation, and more. In regard to the Founding Fathers, I would have been in the camp of the Federalists (e.g., Madison and Hamilton) rather than the anti-Federalists (e.g., Patrick Henry). Growing up, the stories of my parents and grandparents talking about their struggles through the Great Depression had a shaping effect on me; my parents and grandparents were strong FDR supporters because of the New Deal programs that helped them come through that period. And finally, I was part of, and supported, the Civil Rights era of the '60s and beyond. My wife Margaret and I participated on an interfaith basis in many rallies, marches, vigils, petitions, and so forth on behalf of human rights over the years.

My more conservative friends and colleagues will disagree with some of my progressive views, just like our founding fathers had extensive disagreements and debates about the direction of our country. This freedom of expression, along with the freedom of religion, is at the heart of our country's democracy. It is in that spirit that I published this book. I hope to spur continuing dialogue on these important issues of faith, justice, and public policy.

About the Author

Gary Maring is a member of Luther Place Memorial Church, a progressive Lutheran church in Washington, D.C., that has been a leader in advocating and implementing social justice ministries to 'the least of these'. He is among the key founders and a board member of N Street Village, a continuum of programs serving more than 60 percent of DC's population of homeless women. Mr. Maring is also a founder of the national Lutheran Volunteer Corps which places about 150 year long volunteers in social justice agencies in sixteen cities. He is also among the founders of the Steinbruck Center at Luther Place church which teaches and advocates about homelessness and other social justice issues. He discusses through these examples how churches can use their property and financial resources in collaborative ways to do the work of the gospels. He has been a long time advocate for faith-based social justice in the public policy arena. He writes a regular blog on religion, politics, and society, which can be viewed at http://gary-maring.blogspot.com. He is President of Maring Publishing: Faith and Public Policy, LLC in Maryland; the entity under which he publishes blogs, books, and articles. His professional career was in transportation policy in the Federal government so he understands the challenges of the national policy, legislative, and budgeting processes which he discusses in his book in regard to faith and justice issues.

Acknowledgements

I want to thank my dear wife Margaret for bearing with me through the book writing and publishing process and apologize to her for continually monopolizing our computer over this last year.

I particularly want to acknowledge my long time pastor and mentor, Pastor John Steinbruck, who helped me and others at Luther Place see the biblical texts in a whole new way. He taught us the rich traditions of Judaism and the New Testament of welcoming the stranger, the outcast, the excluded of society. Out of that understanding, Luther Place took the bold biblical act of opening the doors to the homeless in the particularly cold winter of 1976 when many were dying. Out of that action of welcoming the stranger emerged the miracle of N Street Village, a continuum of services for homeless women that now serves more than 60 percent of the population of homeless women in DC. Over a period of twenty seven years, Pastor John and his devoted wife, mother, and saint Erna continually led us along this journey when the going was difficult and in the process Luther Place was reborn and today stands as a vibrant congregation dedicated to justice for the homeless as well as in all aspects of society.

This Book is Dedicated to:

My wonderful grandchildren who are early in the process of changing the world:

Micaela Marquez
Paula Marquez
Patrick Maring
Leo Maring
Julian Maring

Gary Maring, President
Maring Publishing:
Faith and Public Policy, LLC,
State of Maryland

Introduction

Those of us in the progressive faith communities seek greater consideration of social justice in our nation's public policies. Two of my favorite theologians, Karen Armstrong and Marcus Borg, remind us that the practice of compassion and justice is central to our Judeo-Christian heritage. Borg says: "A famous passage from the book of Micah is one of the most compact expressions of biblical faith. In a few words it combines the practice of paying attention to God with kindness and justice. Micah asks: What does the Lord require of you? His answer: To do justice, To love kindness, To walk humbly with your God"[3]. At times, our nation seems so far removed from God's biblical call to us in Micah; I use the following compelling national policy issues to illustrate the point:

1.   **The increasing incivility in our political dialogue.** America has the capacity to rise above the hatred, racism, bigotry, xenophobia, and homophobia that we have seen in the political dialogue the last few years; it has only gotten worse during the recent 2011–2012 presidential campaign. I think many would agree that it is time to stop the over-the-top, hateful political language. Even former First Lady Barbara Bush has had enough; she said in early 2012, "It's been, I think, the worst campaign I've ever seen in my life."[4] Equally disturbing are the verbal attacks from the Religious Right[i] who have

i   Note: I use the term Religious Right in my book to include what in the past have been called Fundamentalists and in some cases included evangelicals who

1

denigrated gays, Mormons, Muslims, immigrants, and many others; in so doing, they completely miss the central justice message of the gospels (i.e., compassion for all of God's people, illustrated by the Golden Rule). One of my favorite theologians, Karen Armstrong, says: "We can either emphasize with those aspects of our traditions, religious or secular, that speak of hatred, exclusion, and suspicion, or work with those that stress the interdependence and equality of all human beings.[5]" The choice is ours!

2. **The unholy alliance of the Religious Right and the Political Right.** One of the most disturbing trends to me of all is the unholy marriage of the religious right to the political right in this country. Theologian Brian McLaren, author of a *New Kind of Christianity,* and a leader in the Emerging Church movement, expresses deep concern that here in America, many churches have so identified themselves with American nationalism, and especially with a certain neoconservative ethos in the Republican Party, a kind of partisan alliance that he thinks is dangerous. As a result, he suggests, "the word 'Jesus' now means things it shouldn't mean: judgmental, angry, exclusive, unkind, lacking understanding, reactionary, violent, pro-war, anti-poor, and the like." Later in this section I describe the hateful comments coming out of the Religious Right's so-called Values Voters Summit last fall in DC. It is time for the progressive religious community to stand up against the Religious Right's distortion of our Judeo-Christian heritage.

---

align with them. However the term evangelical has a much broader meaning; my Lutheran church is called the Memorial Evangelical Lutheran Church but we are a part of the progressive mainline denominations (Note: Martin Luther first used the term 'evangelical' to distinguish Protestants from Catholics). Evangelical groups such as Sojourners and The New Evangelical Partnership for the Common Good are progressive partners in advocating for social justice. Many young evangelicals have broken ranks with the more fundamentalist evangelical groups to advocate for social justice, environmental concerns, etc. So it not appropriate to group all evangelicals with the Religious Right.

3.   **The growing income inequality in our country.** Theologian
      Marcus Borg, in his book *Speaking Christian*, says that "the U.S.
      is the most Christian country in the world yet we have the
      greatest income inequality of any of the developed nations.
      Our income inequality is literally off the charts." It is reported
      that the richest four hundred Americans have more wealth
      than half of all American households combined, and in 2010,
      93 percent of income growth went to the wealthiest one
      percent.[6] And at the same time, that income inequality has
      become so skewed, the poverty rate continues to increase
      each year; it's now at 15 percent overall, and for children it is an
      astounding 22 percent.[7] At a time when our country has more
      than one in five children living in poverty, the 2013 House
      budget discussed below proposes to drastically cut food
      stamps, child nutrition programs, Medicaid for the poor, and
      more. The potential for such inequities to lead to broad social
      discord is one of the reasons God's word speaks so clearly
      about the importance of fairness and justice in society.

4.   **Federal and state budget proposals that seek to balance
      budgets on the backs of the neediest in society.** The most
      visible manifestations of this trend are both the 2012 and
      2013 proposed House of Representative's budgets, led by
      Paul Ryan (R., Wisc.). Disguised as deficit-cutting proposals,
      they are largely a transfer of the nation's resources from
      programs for the neediest to the wealthy and corporations
      in the form of tax cuts. Robert Greenstein, president of the
      Center on Budget and Policy Priorities says about the Ryan
      proposal: "It would likely produce the largest redistribution of
      income from the bottom to the top in modern U.S. history and
      likely increase poverty and inequality more than any other
      budget in recent times."[8] These budgets are largely political
      statements guided by the ideology of the political Right. Paul
      Ryan and his Tea Party supporters in the House openly admit
      they are followers of philosopher Ayn Rand, who preaches
      individualism and survival of the fittest. However, we in the

faith communities know that the Bible does not follow Ayn Rand's philosophy. Evangelical scholar Ronald Sider, in his book *Fixing a Moral Deficit*, says: "From one end of the Bible to another, we hear a powerful summons to have a special concern for poor and needy persons." From the Catholic bishops, to progressive evangelical groups like Sojourners, and the mainline denominations, the religious community is beginning to challenge such unjust policies in our society. Concerned members of the religious community have formed an interfaith Circle of Protection to try to protect the most vulnerable in society from such budget assaults.[9]

5. **The challenge to our democracy of "We the people."** The Supreme Court's decision in *Citizens United vs. the Federal Election Commission* paved the way for unlimited corporate spending in elections and the potential drowning out of the average citizen's voice in our public policy debates. The court has made an already bad situation worse by enhancing the ability of the deepest-pocketed special interests to influence elections and the U.S. Congress. As Justice John Paul Stevens explained in dissent, "corporations are not themselves members of 'We the People' by whom and for whom our Constitution was established."[10] And now, a year later, we see the deep-pocketed super donors willing and ready to give far more than the $2,500 checks that regular donors are limited to writing to candidates. Already in 2012 it is reported that about two dozen individuals, couples, or corporations gave $1 million or more to presidential campaign super PACs.[11] It has been reported that the Koch brothers (who together are estimated to have the third richest personal fortune in the world) are planning to raise and spend more than $200 million to defeat President Obama in 2012.[12] And then when I see one billionaire gambling magnate in Las Vegas singlehandedly keeping a presidential candidate (i.e., Newt Gingrich) afloat, I conclude something is radically wrong with our democracy.

By any measure, I don't think this is what the Founding Fathers had in mind.

Current Political Context

In this section of the introduction, I dig a little deeper into the current political state of play. This helps set the context for the remainder of the book.

Political dialogue reached a new low in 2011–2012 as I was writing this book. In March 2011, multiple media sources reported that during a meeting of the Kansas House Appropriations Committee discussing efforts to shoot invasive swine from helicopters, Virgil Peck, Republican state representative, commented to the effect that since shooting these immigrating hogs works, maybe we should apply this solution to our illegal immigration problem.[13] In Alabama, a sponsor of the recent anti-immigration legislation, State Senator Scott Beason, was apparently taped by the FBI talking about black residents of Greene County as aborigines. He is also reported as the lawmaker who urged fellow Republicans to "empty the clip" to stop illegal immigrants.[14][15] Bill James, commissioner of Mecklenburg County, NC, e-mailed his colleagues after Congress repealed Don't Ask, Don't Tell, calling gay people "sexual predators" who would harm U.S. national security if allowed to serve openly in the military.[16] Congressman Alan West (R-Florida) was recently reported to have said at a campaign event in Florida: "I believe there are about 78 to 81 members of the Democratic Party that are members of the Communist Party"; who ever thought we would again revert to the McCarthy era.[17] Right-wing commentator Rush Limbaugh is reported to have recently called poor children receiving the free lunch program in Missouri, "wanton little waifs and serfs dependent on the state."[18] Limbaugh went over the line again on the issue of contraception. After a young law student from Georgetown University, Sandra Fluke, bravely testified on Capitol Hill about how contraceptive services can save women's lives, Limbaugh responded by calling her a "slut" and a "prostitute" and suggested that she and her friends should be required to post sex videos on the Internet.[19] And finally, it was reported that then presidential candidate Rick Santorum implied during a campaign interview that President Obama's policies are following the path of Hitler;[20] is this meant to suggest that Obama's policies are likely to lead to religion-based genocide? I think most would agree that it is time to stop such over-the-top, vitriolic political language. America has always had the capacity to rise above such rancor, hatred, and racism. First and foremost, our politicians should cease using this vitriolic type of language. Then they should commit to calling out such hatred, whenever it appears, as not appropriate to America's tradition. After all, many of these same politicians claim that America is exceptional, so let's prove it.

Meanwhile, fundamentalist and evangelical Christians assembled in Washington DC in late 2011 for their annual Values Voter Summit along with many of the invited Republican presidential candidates. Multiple media sources reported the extreme rhetoric on display at the summit; Muslims, gays, and Mormons were particular targets.[21] Among the values reportedly expressed at the summit are the following (Source: Right Wing Watch):[22]

- The church must rise "like a mighty army" to challenge progressive values, like the repeal of Don't Ask, Don't Tell.
- Gay people are evil and the "homosexual agenda" threatens America's liberty.
- Gay marriage and abortion are the same as slavery and the holocaust, and God will punish America if they continue.
- Gay marriage will destroy America.
- Progressives hate America and legal abortion, LGBT equality and secular government are undermining the country's moral fiber.
- Evolution is evil and if a president endorses the theory of evolution over creationism, the nation will turn into a secular, Nazi-like state.
- Mormons are not Christian and belong to a cult.
- There is no separation of church and state under the Constitution—it's a myth.

Pastor Steven Andrew, president of USA Christian Ministries and author of *Making A Strong Christian Nation*, claimed in a press release early in 2012 that God wants Christians to vote for Rick Santorum. Pastor Andrews says in part that: "Santorum loves God. Romney and Obama don't love God because they don't obey Jesus…Santorum is a Catholic and I am a Christian. There may be some differences, but we have the same God. However, that isn't true with Romney and Obama. Their gods are demons, so they would lead Americans astray."[23]

This rhetoric from the Religious Right seems extremely exclusive and even hateful. I have to say very strongly that this type of language in no way reflects the Judeo-Christian faith tradition that I follow and have been taught. While these fundamentalist Christians are busy attacking those of other religions and lifestyles, they completely miss the central justice message of the gospels (i.e. compassion for the least of these). Income disparity in the United States has reached new heights, yet the Religious Right supports politicians who advocate more tax breaks for the wealthy while advocating national and state budget cuts that often target the most vulnerable in society, despite the fact that these policies are often against the Religious Right's own economic interests.

A recent report by the nonpartisan Congressional Budget Office (CBO) shows that income for households at the higher end of the income scale rose much more rapidly than income for households in moderate to lower income brackets. The report indicates that average real household market income for the highest income group nearly tripled between 1979 and 2007, while income increased by about 19 percent for a household at the midpoint of the income distribution. As a result of that uneven growth, the share of total market income received by the top 1 percent (over seven hundred thousand dollars in annual income) more than doubled between 1979 and 2007, growing from about 10 percent to more than 20 percent. CBO further says: "The precise reasons for the rapid growth in income at the top are not well understood, though researchers have offered several potential rationales…including structure of executive compensation and the increasing scale of financial-sector activities."[24] No wonder citizens were upset about the financial industry bailout in 2008–9 and we saw Occupy Wall Street emerge to protest the financial inequities in our society. The most well-off were bailed out by the average citizen's taxes. Yet recent political discourse about the deficit focuses on spending cuts affecting the most vulnerable while protecting military spending and corporate tax breaks and preserving tax cuts for the wealthy. Free enterprise is a key underpinning of our society, but extreme economic inequities undercut the fabric holding our society together. Meanwhile, the Supreme Court, in the recent infamous *Citizens United* case, gives corporations virtually unlimited power to influence elections and political discourse.

The 2013 House budget proposal led by Congressman Paul Ryan perfectly illustrates the distortion of our national budget priorities. The bipartisan Congressional Budget Office finds that Ryan's 2013 budget plan would cut programs that help low- and middle-income people afford health insurance—Medicaid, Complete Health Improvement Program (CHIP), and the Affordable Care Act's subsidies to help near-poor and moderate-income families afford insurance— by more than 75 percent by 2050, with the bulk of the cuts coming from Medicaid. The huge cuts in so-called mandatory spending would also slash programs like food stamps, welfare, and nutrition programs while giving additional tax reductions to the wealthy and corporations. The Center on Budget and Policy Priorities estimates that 62 percent of cuts come from programs for low-income Americans and 37 percent of the tax benefits go to the few Americans earning more than $1 million. I wonder how Ryan has the gall to call his bill a "Path to Prosperity"? There is not much doubt whose prosperity he is talking about. I'm not sure whether to laugh or cry at such hypocrisy. This seems to be right out of a Dickens novel!

In advance of the Ryan budget release, the United States Conference of Catholic Bishops sent a letter to Congress urging them to adhere to three moral principles when making budget decisions:

1. Every budget decision should be assessed by whether it protects or threatens human life and dignity.
2. A central moral measure of any budget proposal is how it affects "the least of these" (Matthew 25). The needs of those

who are hungry and homeless, without work, or in poverty should come first.

3. Government and other institutions have a shared responsibility to promote the common good of all, especially ordinary workers and families who struggle to live in dignity in difficult economic times.

Sojourners reports that Father Thomas Kelly, a Catholic priest who lives in Ryan's district, raised concerns that the budget Ryan proposed is not consistent with Catholic social teaching. He says:"I'm disappointed by his cruel budget plan and outraged that he defends it on moral grounds. Ryan is Catholic, and he knows that justice for the poor and economic fairness are core elements of our church's social teaching. It's shameful that he disregarded these principles in his budget."[25] Georgetown University (Washington D.C.) faculty and administrators also challenged Representative Ryan for his misuse of Catholic social teaching in defending his budget, which they say hurts the poor. The group sent a letter to Rep. Ryan in advance of his speaking engagement on the Catholic campus. The scholars are also reported to have given the Representative a reading assignment: "The Compendium of the Social Doctrine of the Church"![26] The House had the opportunity to vote on a much more balanced and effective deficit plan than that of Ryan and his colleagues, the one developed by the Simpson Bowles Deficit Commission, but it was voted down overwhelmingly.

Meanwhile, the news about poverty levels in America is bleak. The richest nation in the world has the highest poverty level of any Western industrialized nation.[27] The Bureau of the Census reports "that the nation's official poverty rate in 2010 was 15.1 percent, up from 14.3 percent in 2009 — the third consecutive annual increase in the poverty rate. There were 46.2 million people in poverty in 2010, up from 43.6 million in 2009 — the fourth consecutive annual increase and the largest number in the 52 years for which poverty estimates have been published." Further, the poverty rate increased for children to 22.0 percent in 2010.[28] This comes at a time when many of the programs that would help those in poverty are on the chopping block in federal and state budgets, under the guise of cutting deficits.

At the end of the 1990s, we had benefitted from one of the best decades of economic growth on record, and we actually had a federal budget surplus. Only eight years later, we were in the worst recession since the Great Depression, incurring trillion dollar annual deficits. Ronald Sider in his new book *Fixing the Moral Deficit*, says that about half of the total $20 trillion that the federal government will owe by 2019 results from the wars in Iraq and Afghanistan and from the Bush-era tax cuts, which were all initiated early in his presidency without offsets that are normally required in the budgeting process. The policies look so tragic in hindsight as we sit in 2012 and see how futile these wars were in creating democracy and how futile the tax cuts were in spurring economic growth over the last decade, while both contributed mightily to the deficits we now face. If only we had finished the removal of al-Qaeda immediately after 9/11 rather than taking the unwarranted detour into Iraq where there was no al-Qaeda threat and no weapons of mass destruction as claimed. (Note: Only recently did we come back to dismantling the al-Qaeda threat, with the killing of Osama bin Laden and many of his key leaders, who were mostly in Pakistan.) Our country would be so much more financially healthy today, and we would have avoided all the tragic loss of life and long-term disabilities of our own troops, as well as the millions killed and displaced in Iraq and Afghanistan, had we not pursued such flawed national policies. I have great admiration for the soldiers who fought these wars, but with many in their fourth deployments to Iraq or Afghanistan, we have clearly pushed then beyond a reasonable call to duty. We owe it to our loyal soldiers to take much more seriously the terrible decision of when to go war. And we in the religious community are called to be peacemakers and only drawn into war when it is truly a last resort. The Just War Theory, developed by Saint Thomas Aquinas in the thirteenth century, can guide us in this regard. Many in the faith community completely abandoned their religious teaching in supporting the rush to war in Iraq. We must never let this happen again.

Human and civil rights issues continue to be at the forefront of national policy. During the last couple years and into this important political campaign season, we have seen a proliferation of state laws to try to limit voter registration for minority groups under the guise of voter identification (ID). Several of these laws have been challenged by the Justice Department, but the outcome is not clear at this point. Women's rights have been at the forefront of the Republican primary campaign, with Rick Santorum seemingly wanting to reverse progress in contraception and family planning made over the last fifty years in this country. Many conservative, male-dominated state legislatures have initiated laws to put restrictions on women's reproductive rights such as personhood laws and vaginal ultrasound requirements for women who want to consider an abortion. Anti-immigrant and anti-Sharia laws have popped up in several states as well; the former being a significant affront to many Hispanics, and the latter being a clear affront to American Muslims. 'Birther' hysteria has proliferated since the election of Barack Obama in 2008. Much of this is likely racial and xenophobic in origin and not unrelated to our country having its first African American president, who many of the Religious and Political Right suspect to be Muslim.

So where are the progressive voices in politics, society, and religion to challenge these tragic policies in areas of economics, war, and human rights? President Obama and the progressive members within the Democratic Party seem to have lost their voices, and the Republican presidential candidates seem to be outdoing themselves to cater to the base of the party, which tends to be anti-immigrant, anti gay, anti-government, anti-tax, anti-health reform, and the list goes on. Historically, the great U.S. presidents of both parties reached beyond selfish interests to adopt some of the most progressive ideas and laws any nation has ever seen; they moved the country toward ensuring justice for all. By most accounts, the greatest presidents are Washington, who oversaw implementation of our nation's Constitution and Bill of Rights; Lincoln; who issued the Emancipation Proclamation; Franklin Delano Roosevelt, who implemented the New Deal; Thomas Jefferson, the main author of the Declaration of Independence; and Teddy Roosevelt, a Progressive who challenged the so-called corporate robber barons of his day, recommended progressive income tax and estate taxes on the wealthy, and launched the first federal efforts on environmental conservation including the national parks). And these progressive periods were often supported by faith communities, such as the Quakers, who advocated for abolition of slavery in Lincoln's time. The Social Gospel movement early in the twentieth century was instrumental in forming the Progressive Party in 1912 and helped to craft the party's social reform agenda of fair wages, workplace regulations, social security and unemployment measures, national health care, conservation, and industrial reform. And the Catholic Worker Movement, which promoted social justice policies for workers and others during the depression, is another example of a faith movement that supported a progressive political period.

In regard to the role of the churches in social justice today, Chris Hedges, a Pulitzer Prize–winning journalist, in his book, *Death of the Liberal Class*, comes down hard on the liberal church and its pastors: He says in a recent blog post that, "The liberal church forgot that heretics exist. It forgot that the scum of society always wrap themselves in the flag and clutch the Christian cross to promote programs that mock the core teachings of Jesus Christ. And, for all their years of seminary training and Bible study, these liberal clergy have stood by mutely as televangelists betrayed and exploited the Gospel to promote bigotry, hatred and greed. What was the point, I wonder, of ordination? Did they think the radical message of the Gospel was something they would never have to fight for?"

He goes on to say: "Churches and pastors who stood for Civil Rights in the 1960s, marched with Martin Luther King and fought against the likes of the Ku Klux Klan are nowhere to be seen today as bigots and xenophobes posing as Christians attack the very fabric of our democratic pluralistic society." The likes of Glenn Beck attack progressive churches and the concept of social justice with hardly a peep from the mainline churches. Hedges further says; we "Let hate speech pollute the airways. Let corporations buy up your courts and state and federal legislative bodies. Let the Christian religion be manipulated by charlatans to demonize Muslims, gays and intellectuals, discredit science and become a source of personal enrichment."[29]

This is probably an overly harsh indictment of the church and its leaders, but it does raise a concern that the progressive voice of the church seems to have been silenced. My own congregation, Luther Place, is one of the exceptions; it took on the issue of homelessness in the 1970s, when few other churches or government agencies seemed to care. It stands as a witness to what churches can do with their property and financial resources to serve the neediest in society. Further, successfully creating this social justice ministry gave us the credibility to advocate for just treatment and funding from local and national government officials on behalf of the homeless and other disadvantaged.

Jim Wallis of the Sojourners organization, in his book *The Great Awakening*, says that "two of the great hungers in our world today are the hunger for spirituality and the hunger for social justice. The connection between the two is the one the world is waiting for, especially the new generation. And the first will empower the second." At the same time, he sees a significant emerging dynamic both within institutional churches and more secular spiritual movements, which I will discuss further in the book. The emergence and potential coming together of these movements could portend another Great Awakening in our country.

Robert Jones, in his book *Progressive and Religious*, suggests that the heart of the religious life should not only be personal piety but also addressing structural injustice. But believers have too often buried the voice of the prophets, presumably because the social justice issues they raise are too uncomfortable to deal with. Instead, we tend to see contemporary religion mostly focused on personal salvation, largely ignoring the justice aspect of faith. In his book *Meeting Jesus Again for the First Time*, Marcus Borg strips Jesus of much of the post-resurrection doctrine that has been laid on over the centuries; in the process, a different image of Jesus begins to emerge. Borg emphasizes that Jesus' pre-Easter ministry was largely focused on compassion and justice on behalf of the oppressed. This was very subversive to the religious authorities of the time, who defined culture based on a purity system. Their definition of purity drew strict social and economic lines of who was in and out, and the religious and civil authorities were upset by the inclusiveness that Jesus displayed in eating with those who were considered the untouchables. He attracted enemies, especially among the rich and powerful, and it eventually got him crucified. Similar 'purity' lines are drawn in current society regarding issues like homosexuality, the homeless, immigrants, and so forth. But Jesus' message (and that of the other great biblical prophets) and example call us to stand with the oppressed of our time.

What I see today is a need for rejuvenation of the progressive spirit in America to counter the more fundamentalist trends that, if followed, would take us back to a period before the 1960s Civil Rights Movement when the white majority was dominant, women knew their place in the home, and minorities were suppressed. Many young people have turned away from organized religion, but there is a large spirituality movement that has much in common with more traditional progressive church values. Many are turned off by members of the Religious Right who have captured too much of the current religious media's attention with such negative rhetoric. We in the progressive religious community need to find ways to connect with today's spiritual movement, social justice oriented evangelicals, and secular progressives.. We have the great examples of the Social Gospel movement and Catholic social teaching that played influential roles in the progressive search for economic fairness and justice in the early part of the twentieth century. Both traditions promoted the belief that any true commitment to the Gospels and the example of Jesus Christ demanded followers to take concrete steps to address oppression and hardship in this world. Where and when will the prophetic voices and leaders arise in our nation, the present-day equivalents of Dorothy Day, Harriet Beecher Stowe, and Martin Luther King?

As mentioned at the beginning of this section, there are many important social and political issues of the day at both the local and national level that desperately need a progressive, social justice oriented action agenda through bringing together the faithful, spiritual, and secular justice-oriented communities. We like to think of our country as particularly blessed by God and exceptional among nations. Yet a recent report evaluating social justice among developed countries shows the United States to be among the lower tier of countries on justice indicators, particularly due to our country's high poverty levels.[30] Economic justice is an increasingly important issue, as the growing gap in income between the wealthy and the average worker threatens the American dream. Further, the tendency for federal and state budget cuts to be targeted to programs helping society's most vulnerable needs to be much more aggressively challenged by both secular and religious progressives. Organizations such as Faith in Public Life and the Network of Spiritual Progressives (of which I am a member) have emerged to help fill this void, but the conservative mix of political and corporate interests and the Religious Right still command inordinate influence. Sojourners, the New Evangelical Partnership for the Common Good and the Evangelicals for Social Action are among evangelical organizations which advocate for many of the same justice issues the progressive faith communities are advocating, are a hopeful sign; this opens up further partnering opportunities.

For this book, I have reviewed more than thirty key books, plus other articles, written by leading theologians and scholars of our day (see appendix A) who describe the unprecedented changes taking place in religion, provide a refocusing of the justice message of the biblical texts, and discuss implications for society and public policy. This review is supplemented with citations from key writers and scholars who describe our most important national and global public policy challenges. Out of the insights gained from these best minds of our day and my own faith and social justice experiences, I describe a possible vision for the progressive faithful and spiritual communities to help bring biblical social justice concepts to today's public policy debate.

❶
Historical Progressive Movements

Our forefathers were enlightened statesmen; most had spent time in Europe in ambassador positions or on other missions to better understand different forms of governments and the revolutionary spirit that was happening there. Many of these ideas were incorporated by Jefferson, Madison, and Hamilton in the Declaration of Independence, the Bill of Rights, and the Constitution. The Declaration of Independence most famously says: "We hold these truths to be self-evident, that *all men are created equal,* that they are endowed by their Creator with certain unalienable Rights, that among these are *Life, Liberty and the pursuit of Happiness.*" Alexis de Tocqueville, a young French nobleman and political scientist who visited America in 1832, was inspired to write in *Democracy in America* that the foundering democracy he observed in America "is a bold and hopeful experiment in fostering equality of mankind." He further observed that America's democracy at the time had many imperfections, but it had many advantages for individual opportunity, initiative, freedom, and justice over the aristocratic regimes of the Old World.[31]

As an aside, I find it interesting that Conservatives, particularly Tea Party members, regularly refer to the intent of our nation's founders and the Constitution in regard to their political agenda. I have studied *The Federalist Papers*, *The Anti-Federalist Papers*, and the ratification process for the Constitution. There is no doubt in my mind that these small-government, state's-right Conservatives would have been the anti-Federalists who opposed adoption of the

Constitution. Alexander Hamilton, who wrote most of the *Federalist Papers* making the case for ratification of the Constitution, was a proponent of a strong central government. James Madison of Virginia, who received the title of "Father of the Constitution" and also wrote a number of the *Federalist Papers*, was a strong advocate for the Constitution as a replacement for the Articles of Confederation, which had resulted in a weak and ineffective federal government. So anytime you hear a politician wanting to go back to the founders and the Constitution, tell them, "That's great, because the Declaration of Independence, the Bill of Rights, and the Constitution are some of the most progressive governing documents ever written," as cited by de Tocqueville above. As an example of misinterpreting the Constitution, presidential candidate Ron Paul is reported to have recently said that the Constitution was written explicitly to restrain the federal government.[32] In fact, the framers did exactly the opposite; they greatly strengthened the national government and weakened the states precisely because the Articles of Confederation, with the heavy tilt toward state's rights, proved unworkable in practice. Since that time the federal government, underpinned by its Constitutional role, has greatly improved human rights for all the nation; invested in the nation's infrastructure such as railroads, canals, and the Interstate Highway System for improved interstate commerce; and led us through the Civil War, the emancipation of slaves, women's suffrage, the Great Depression, the Civil Rights movement, vital social programs for the common good, critical research and technology, space-age advancements, global leadership in economics and security, and more.

In regard to the founders and religion, they were enlightened and were very intentional about religious freedom and the separation of government and religion. Those suggesting our founders never intended separation of church and state are way off base. Creation of the federal Constitution essentially resulted in the disestablishment of state religions. Most of the state constitutions written immediately after the American Revolution supported Christianity in some way and often imposed some form of religious test for holding office including support for established Anglican (now Episcopal) religion, as in Virginia's state constitution. Jefferson pushed for both the disestablishment of the Anglican church in Virginia and the enactment of The Virginia Statute for Religious Freedom. He was a deist and was not a member of any institutional religion. He even went so far as to create a Jefferson Bible (currently on display at the Smithsonian) in which he removed from the Gospels the miracles, the Virgin birth, and the resurrection of Jesus, leaving only what he deemed the moral philosophy of Jesus. In this light, how do fundamentalists claim our Founding Fathers, including Jefferson, intended to establish a Christian nation?

Madison was also instrumental in getting The Virginia Statute for Religious Freedom passed. Madison and Jefferson's influence carried through in eventual drafting of the Constitution, including the First Amendment provisions for religious freedom. Following ratification, many critics felt the Constitution was godless, and in some critic's minds it seemed anti-God, since Article 6, Section 3 forbids any religious test for holding office. It was feared that an atheist might become president. It was also felt by some that the nation needed God's protection during wartime, and they made attempts to rewrite the Preamble to the Constitution to declare America a Christian nation. These efforts failed, but later, during the Civil War, Salmon P. Chase, Secretary of the Treasury, put "In God We Trust" on America's money. In the Cold War, "Under God" was added to the Pledge of Allegiance.[33] These efforts continue, for example, with the attempts to put the Ten Commandments in public places. Rick Santorum continually questions separation of church and state, even criticizing John F. Kennedy's famous speech on this topic, saying that upon reading Kennedy's speech again, it made him want to throw up! Here, in part, is what Kennedy said:

I believe in an America...

- that is officially neither Catholic, Protestant nor Jewish; where no public official either requests or accepts instructions on public policy from the Pope, the National Council of Churches or any other ecclesiastical source;

- where no religious body seeks to impose its will directly or indirectly upon the general populace or the public acts of its officials; and
- where religious liberty is so indivisible that an act against one church is treated as an act against all.

For while this year it may be a Catholic against whom the finger of suspicion is pointed, in other years it has been, and may someday be again, a Jew—or a Quaker or a Unitarian or a Baptist. It was Virginia's harassment of Baptist preachers, for example, that helped lead to Jefferson's statute of religious freedom. Today I may be the victim, but tomorrow it may be you—until the whole fabric of our harmonious society is ripped at a time of great national peril.

Finally, I believe in an America where...

- religious intolerance will someday end; where all men and all churches are treated as equal;
- where every man has the same right to attend or not attend the church of his choice;
- where there is no Catholic vote, no anti-Catholic vote, no bloc voting of any kind; and
- where Catholics, Protestants and Jews, at both the lay and pastoral level, will refrain from those attitudes of disdain and division which have so often marred their works in the past, and promote instead the American ideal of brotherhood.[34]

While some claim Kennedy may have gone too far to separate religion and government, there is a lot to be said positively about the speech. Many people, including me, were truly offended by what Santorum said about it. His commentary only illustrates the extent to which the Religious and Political Right want to impose their so-called family (religious) values on the general populace. On the issues of contraception and family planning, for example, society has largely accepted them for both economic and health reasons. Further, both women and men expect to have insurance coverage for such matters and this is particularly vital for poorer women. The Catholic Health

Association, representing Catholic hospitals and led by Sister Carol Keehan, supported the original Obama led health care legislation and the recently announced compromise on contraceptive coverage even though the U.S. Catholic Bishops did not.[35] My church (the ELCA) "supports the development and use of medical products, birth control, and initiatives that support fulfilling and responsible sexuality...[and] recognizes the important role that the availability of birth control has played in allowing women and men to make responsible decisions about the bearing and rearing of children."[36]

Presidents of both parties have led progressive periods in history. Abraham Lincoln was the first Republican president, and he was one of this country's greatest presidents, as well as a very progressive one. During the Civil War, the Lincoln administration greatly expanded the role of the national government in the economy and in the fight against the Confederacy, creating a national banking system, adopting an income tax, creating the Department of Agriculture, and adopting a draft. Lincoln argued that the national government held sway over the states and used the implied war powers in the Constitution to free the slaves in the South under the Emancipation Proclamation. After meeting Frederick Douglass, Lincoln allowed African Americans to serve in the Union armies, and as he saw their valor in battle, Lincoln grew stronger as an advocate of African Americans' civil rights. He set up the Freedman's Bureau for the freed slaves and lobbied for the Thirteenth Amendment, which would permanently abolish slavery in the whole nation.[37] Quakers played a major role in the abolition movement against slavery. The Quakers were the first whites to denounce slavery in the American colonies and Europe. Harriet Beecher Stowe, writing from a faith perspective, was instrumental in swaying public opinion against slavery with the publication of *Uncle Tom's Cabin* in 1851. Jim Wallis says in his book, *The Great Awakening,* "Christians helped lead the abolitionist struggle, efforts to end child labor, projects to aid working people and establish unions, and even the battle to obtain voting rights for women. Here were evangelical Christians fighting for social justice, precisely because of what God had done for them."

As mentioned in my introduction, the 1890s to the 1920s was a significant progressive period of social activism and reform. One main goal of this movement was government reform, as they tried to eliminate corruption. Women's suffrage was promoted, as was achieving efficiency in every sector by identifying old ways that needed modernizing and emphasizing scientific, medical, and engineering solutions. Progressives drew support from the middle class, and supporters included many lawyers, teachers, physicians, ministers and business people. They followed advances underway at the time in Europe and adopted numerous policies, such as the banking laws that became the foundation for the Federal Reserve System in 1914. Republican President Teddy Roosevelt (1901–1909) was a key champion of this progressive movement. Roosevelt developed a philosophy that became known as the Square Deal, which expanded the government's regulatory powers over private industry. Roosevelt felt that a strong federal government with strong regulatory powers was necessary to restrain corporate excess.[38] Roosevelt, after losing the Republican presidential nomination in 1912, ran on a new Progressive party ticket in the1912 presidential election. According to the Center for American Progress, "Proponents of the social gospel were instrumental in forming the Progressive Party in 1912 and helped to craft the party's social reform agenda of fair wages, workplace regulations, social security and unemployment measures, national health care, conservation, and industrial reform. These social gospel progressives pressed notions of brotherhood and social solidarity above individualism and greed, and paved the way for significant legislative reforms during the Wilson and Roosevelt presidencies."

Progressive religious leaders, such as Catholic Priest John Ryan and the Catholic bishops, were important to this movement with publication of the *Program of Social Reconstruction* in 1919, which advocated for worker rights, housing, social insurance, and more. Further, Dorothy Day and Peter Maurin created the Catholic Worker Movement in 1933 during the height of the depression. They sought to provide direct support for the poor (mostly in urban areas) and to encourage a larger Catholic ethic of nonviolence, concern for human dignity, and solidarity with the least well-off.[39]

FDR's New Deal era was another great progressive period. The New Deal was a series of economic programs and legislation in response to the Great Depression. It included the Wagner Act to promote labor unions, the Works Progress Administration (WPA) relief program, the Social Security Act, and it saw the creation of the United States Housing Authority and Farm Security Administration and the Fair Labor Standards Act of 1938, which set maximum hours and minimum wages for most categories of workers.

I witnessed the 1960s progressive period firsthand. The Great Society programs of the mid sixties included major accomplishments such as the Civil Rights Act of 1964, the Voting Rights Act of 1965, new housing programs, and the enactment of Medicare for seniors. The mainline progressive churches played an important role in the civil rights movement. Many pastors and laypeople went south to march against segregation with Martin Luther King Jr.

When I graduated from Pennsylvania State University in 1964, I began a career with the federal government, at the U.S. Department of Transportation. In 1967, my federal job brought me to Washington DC, where I served the remainder of my career in transportation policy. In those early years in DC, I witnessed some of the progressive accomplishments mentioned above, as well as some of the great tragedies and challenges of our nation, including the assassinations of Martin Luther King Jr. (MLK) and Bobby Kennedy in 1968, the riots and burnings in DC following MLK's assassination, and the huge protests against the Vietnam War. The country has tended more conservative since 1980, and there have been multiple attempts to roll back New Deal and Great Society programs. Other than deregulation in the 1980s, most of the progressive-era programs have remained largely intact. However, recent deficit concerns have again brought programs like Medicare, Medicaid, and Social Security to the forefront for possible reform, including the introduction of proposals for privatization that have been very controversial.

Regarding the role of faith in these progressive movements, the Center for American Progress in its October 2010 report, "The Role of Faith in the Progressive Movement," says:

A...powerful strand of progressive thought emerged directly from religious values during the social gospel movement. These reformers argued that Christians should apply their teachings to public problems. American Protestant ministers and theologians during the 19th century such as Walter Rauschenbusch espoused this belief, as did politicians such as William Jennings Bryan, and settlement founders such as Jane Addams and Ellen Gates Starr. Catholic social justice leaders such as Fr. John Ryan and Dorothy Day pushed for similar values and religious activism, and later civil rights leaders such as Dr. Martin Luther King, Jr. followed suit. Many of the most prominent social movements in American progressive history would not have been possible without the inspirational values and moral authority of socially conscious Christianity and Judaism...Progressives working within these faith traditions applied religious morality to the task of transforming American society during the industrial age away from the exploitation of workers and toward more cooperative forms of economic life. These faith-driven progressives insisted that society and governments uphold the fundamental notion that all people are equal in God's eyes and deserve basic dignity, freedom, political rights, and economic opportunities in life. Religious progressives promoted the notion of community and solidarity above concepts of individualism and materialism, and worked to stop unnecessary wars and military aggression across the globe.

The social gospel movement and Catholic social teaching played influential roles in the progressive search for economic fairness and justice in the 20th century. Both traditions promoted the belief that any true commitment to the Gospels and the example of Jesus Christ demanded followers to take concrete steps to address oppression and hardship in this world and to replace the laissez-faire attitudes of the late 19th century with a more communitarian outlook. In his famous book, *Progress and Poverty*, Henry George, a popular economist and social gospel adherent, rejected the traditional notion of religion that allowed the "rich Christian to bend on Sundays in a nicely upholstered pew...without any feeling of responsibility for the squalid misery that is festering but a square away."[40]

It is clear that no one political party or religious group can claim credit for the progressive movements in U.S. history. Republican Presidents Abraham Lincoln and Teddy Roosevelt led progressive movements during their presidencies, whereas the Democratic administrations of FDR, and Kennedy/Johnson led to implementation of the progressive New Deal, Civil Rights legislation, and the Great Society programs.

2

The Shift Right in Contemporary Politics and Religion

Political Trends

As mentioned in the introduction, political dialogue reached a new low in recent months. State legislators were quoted talking about shooting illegal immigrants, state legislation to adopt anti-Sahria laws was proposed, birther bills that would require presidential candidates to provide proof of citizenship satisfactory to state authorities were drafted, and policies denying rights and services to those in gay marriages were discussed. Prejudice is on display among presidential candidates as well. Then presidential candidate Herman Cain took a position that any community has the right to prohibit Muslims from building a mosque, despite the fact that freedom of religion is a basic tenet of the Constitution. Political analyst Eugene Robinson commented that as an African American, Cain should remember the restrictive Jim Crow laws of the '50s and '60s from when he was growing up.[41] Michele Bachmann became the first presidential candidate to sign a pledge by the Family Leader, an influential social-conservative group in Iowa, which among other things says, "Homosexuality is a choice, a health risk, and can be compared to polygamy or adultery, sex is better after marriage, and Sharia law should be banned. The pledge also states: "Slavery had a disastrous impact on African-American families, yet sadly a child born into slavery in 1860 was more likely to be raised by his mother and father in a two-parent household than was an African-American baby born after the election of the USA's first African-American President."[42] This was a sad start to the 2011-2012 presidential campaign season.

Congressional scholar Norman Ornstein of the conservative American Enterprise Institute has been getting a lot of media attention with a new book, *It's Even Worse Than It Looks: How the American Constitutional System Collided With the New Politics of Extremism*, (co-authored by Thomas Mann) that says about our political system that which was previously unmentionable in polite conversations. They say our political dysfunction is largely because of the transformation of the Republican Party into an extremist force that is "An insurgent outlier... unpersuaded by conventional understanding of facts, evidence and science; dismissive of the legitimacy of its political opposition; and all but declaring war on government."[43] This is manifest in actions such as Majority Leader Mitch McConnell stating that their party's number one priority was to make President Obama a one term President; no matter the very serious state of the economy and other critical national priorities. It was further manifest in the recent defeat of Senator Lugar in an Indiana Republican primary contest with a Tea Party candidate who attacked Lugar for being too bipartisan over his many years in the Senate; this is a significant loss to the Republican Party and to the nation. Economist Paul Krugman argues that this disarray in our political system has been largely caused by the power and money of a small, wealthy minority pursuing their own interests and that the key to recovery lies in finding a way to get past this malign influence.[44]

Former Governor of Michigan, Jennifer Granholm, recently wrote about her dad and the Republican primary: "Dad couldn't care less about legislating access to women's contraception or ordering vaginal ultrasound probes—the very subjects make him uncomfortable. He cares about rational economic policy. But his party has left him, gone to tea."[45] This makes a nice transition to discussing the emergence of the Tea Party. Let us not be fooled by the seeming sincerity of some more moderate Tea Party members. Sean Wilentz in a 2010 New Yorker article claims that underneath the Tea Party umbrella are some fairly extreme elements (e.g., remnants of the John Birch Society) who subscribe to the likes of W. Cleon Skousen. He comments that in 1981, Skousen released the book, *The 5,000 Year Leap*, which relies on selective and questionable assertions to claim that the U.S. Constitution is rooted in the Bible; it also claims that the framers believed in minimal central government.[46] In another of his books, *The Making of America*, Skousen makes controversial claims about slavery and refers to slave children as 'pickaninnies'. In the fall of 2007, Glenn Beck, a Skousen follower, began promoting *The 5,000 Year Leap* on his show, describing it as "divinely inspired," along with the Constitution.[47] These assertions by Skousen and Beck would have astounded James Madison, a framer of the Constitution, who rejected state-established religions and, like Alexander Hamilton, proposed a strong central government to overcome the weaknesses of the Articles of Confederation. As one who has read both the *Federalist Papers* and the *Anti-Federalist Papers*, to me the present day Tea Party advocates of limited government are clearly in the anti-Federalist camp, which argued against our nation adopting the Constitution.

Another Tea Party favorite, author F.A. Hayek, says in regard to liberty and equality: "Not only has liberty nothing to do with any other sort of equality, but it is even bound to produce inequality in many respects. This is the necessary result and part of the justification of individual liberty: if the result of individual liberty did not demonstrate that some manners of living are more successful than others, much of the case for it would vanish."[48] So, let the powerful have their due, and those left behind can eat the crumbs, if there are any.

I wonder why the Tea Party is so concerned about the deficits under President Obama while being so mum under the Bush administration when it took us into two unfunded wars costing trillions of dollars, all off budget; enacted trillion-dollar tax cuts without revenue offsets; expanded Medicare drug benefits without paying for them; enacted TARP bailout for the banks; and other budget busting. You have to believe that part of the outrage that suddenly emerged after Obama took office is based on racism; how else do you explain the crazy birther movement, the Take Back America coalition, the highly charged anti-immigration movement; and the labeling of Obama as a socialist, communist, Muslim, Hitler-like leader, and so on.

The Tea Party's record, so far, is very mixed. During 2011, the Tea Party legislators endangered the nation's credit rating by taking us to the brink of default over raising the debt ceiling; they refused to go along with a debt-reduction plan that their own Majority Leader Boehner had tentatively negotiated with President Obama, and they fought against an extension of unemployment insurance and payroll tax deductions for ordinary Americans while continually railing against any tax increases on wealthy Americans and corporations. They seem to believe that any compromise would bring rebellion from their right-wing followers, so they fight even their own majority leader. A recent example of how the Tea Party is beholden to the right wing came when Rep. Darrell Issa (R, California), gave an interview to the Wall Street Journal in which he suggested that he might further the Conservative agenda through an occasional compromise. That provoked an outburst from Rush Limbaugh, which then produced angry e-mails and phone calls to Issa's office. Issa quickly apologized to Limbaugh and promised only opposition to President Obama.[49]

Glenn Beck, in concert with his rant about the country moving toward socialism, launched an attack on churches that promote social justice. I am proud to say that I am a member of a church that has social justice in its mission and takes that commitment seriously (e.g., by establishing N Street Village for homeless women). If Beck and his followers want to refer to helping the needy as socialism, so be it; let's have more. After all, helping those in need is what the biblical prophets all the way down through Jesus taught us to do. Although individual charity toward the needy is important, our Judeo-Christian heritage suggests there is also a governmental role, which is counter to the minimal-government libertarian strains within the Tea Party. As Jim Wallis of the Sojourners stated in a recent article regarding the Tea Party:

> Serving the poor is clearly a Christian command, but advocating justice for the poor and oppressed is also a biblical calling, as multiple biblical passages suggest. The biblical

prophets, in their condemnations of injustice to the poor, frequently follow those statements by requiring the king (the government) to act justly (a requirement that applied both to the kings of Israel and to foreign potentates). Jeremiah, speaking of King Josiah, wrote, "He defended the cause of the poor and needy, and so all went well" (22:16). Amos instructs the courts (the government) to "Hate evil, love good; maintain justice in the courts" (5:15). Clearly the prophets hold kings, rulers, judges, and employers accountable to the demands of justice. Individuals, families, and congregations are needed to minister to the "least of these," but the Bible says that kings, rulers, judges, employers, and governments also are held biblically accountable to the requirements of justice.[50]

Columnist David Campbell writes, based on his analysis, that the Tea Party roots are not really what many claim, which is that the Tea Party has been radicalized by the recession, government stimulus, and bailout efforts. The analysis shows that today's Tea Party supporters were highly partisan Conservatives long before the Tea Party was born, and that they are overwhelmingly white, have a low regard for immigrants and blacks, and seek to put God more prominently in government.[51] The Pew Research Center's Forum on Religion & Public Life finds that the Tea Party supporters tend to have conservative opinions not just about economic matters, but also about social issues such as abortion and same-sex marriage. In addition, they are much more likely than registered voters on the whole to say that their religion is the most important factor in determining their opinions on these social issues. And they draw disproportionate support from the ranks of the Religious Right. [52] This makes for a good transition into the next section on fundamentalist religious trends.

Fundamentalist Religious Trends

Within the three major monotheistic religions of the world, Christianity, Judaism, and Islam, there has been a disturbing trend toward fundamentalism; a turning back in some cases to medieval times. Historian and theologian Karen Armstrong says, "The fact that fundamentalism has erupted in almost all cultures indicates a widespread and worrying disenchantment with modern society, which so many of us experience as liberating, exciting and empowering."[53]

For example, within Islam, we have witnessed dangerous fundamentalist trends in recent years, much of which is underwritten by Arab governments using oil money we send their way. According to Thomas Madden, in his book *Empires of Trust,* the Islamic concept of jihad comes from essentially a medieval perspective within Islam. He claims that fundamentalist Islamists focus on the Middle Ages, the time when it constituted both a faith and an empire. The great Ottoman Empire ruled much of the world under Islamic law, or Sharia. Remaining parts of the world were thought to be occupied by infidels and unbelievers on whom Islam waged war. Today, the presence of Western infidels in their holy land of the Middle East is viewed as an insult by fundamentalist Muslims, and some like al-Qaeda have turned to killing the infidels. Of course, faith based killing is a total perversion of the core message of compassion within all three of the world's major monotheistic religions. Modern democracies must build tolerance for all their peoples. Turkey and Indonesia are often mentioned as kind of "role models" for the Middle East countries to pattern themselves after. The current revolutions in the Middle East give hope for the future, but transitions to democracy can be difficult, as we saw happen after the Iranian Revolution.

Theologian Harvey Cox says that Christian fundamentalism largely started in the United States. In 1910, in response to a progressive trend in society and religion, antimodernists published a series of booklets call *The Fundamentals*, which contained five nonnegotiable beliefs:

1. The total inerrancy of the Bible
2. The Virgin Birth
3. Substitutionary atonement of Christ on the cross for the sins of the world
4. Resurrection from the dead
5. Imminent second coming

Cox points out that the choice of these five seems arbitrary. There was no mention, for example, of the feeding of the hungry or healing the sick, the parables, or the Sermon on the Mount, all of which portray a social-justice-oriented ministry of Jesus. How fundamentalists can believe in literal reading of the Bible and yet ignore the predominant social justice theme of the biblical texts is beyond me. Former Episcopal bishop and author John Shelby Spong asks how literalists would deal with a passage in which the prophet Samuel (in God's name) instructs Saul, as the king of the Jews, to engage in a war of genocide against the Amalekites, in which he is instructed to kill every man, woman, and child (1 Samuel 15:1-9) or a psalm suggesting that the people of Israel would not be happy until they had dashed the heads of their Babylonian enemies' children against the rocks (Ps. 137:8-9)? [54]

Author Gary Wills points out that early in the twentieth century, the Fundamentalists had their time in the sun, achieving such milestones as Prohibition and the banning of teaching about Darwin in the schools. But the political disaster of the Scopes Trial over teaching evolution and the repeal of Prohibition were serious setbacks for Fundamentalists. [55] As a reaction to the Civil Rights era of the 1960s, fundamentalism again raised its head. Leaders such as Jerry Falwell (who opposed Martin Luther King's protest marches) with the Moral Majority and Pat Robertson with the Christian Coalition had a resurgence in the 1980s. Author Karen Armstrong suggests that only about 10 percent of the U.S. population would today describe itself as fundamentalist, but she believes a much larger segment of the population harbors similar attitudes. [56]

Fundamentalism has had an interesting political journey. At the turn of the twentieth century, a fundamentalist named William Jennings Bryant ran for president three times as the Democratic Party nominee (1896, 1900, 1908) and lost all three times to Republicans. Conversely, the latest affiliation of the fundamentalists is with the Republican Party. This alliance was largely orchestrated by Karl Rove, a political strategist who was instrumental in getting George W. Bush elected; during the early years of the administration, this religious alliance was used as a political tool for conservative social initiatives and war support. Author Gary Wills concludes that just as with the early twentieth century overreach by fundamentalists that ended badly for them, this latest foray of religion into politics has proven to be a disaster.[57] The Bush administration, supported by the right wing 'neocons', (including the Christian Right) rushed to war in Iraq using trumped up charges of weapons of mass destruction virtually stopped vital stem cell research, and wrecked the balanced budget presented by the outgoing Clinton Administration. Enactment of tax cuts favoring the wealthy and funding two wars off budget resulted in a deficit, which left the country in a disastrous economic and budget situation at the end of the Bush Administration. Time and again, religion was used for political motives that often went against Biblical concepts of justices and against the Christian fundamentalists' own economic interests in many cases. The founders must be turning over in their graves at this distorted intermixing of religion and government policy.

Martin Marty, in the *Collision of Faiths*, says that fundamentalism in America came with the threat of the stranger, that is, the influx of immigrants of different cultures and religions. Rather than welcoming the stranger, which is biblical tradition, fundamentalists try to wall themselves off from the stranger. For a long time, he says, groups like Orthodox Jews or ultraconservative Amish were able to keep in their own enclaves and were not normally thought of as fundamentalists. But as the world closed in, fundamentalists in each of the faiths could not effectively filter out these perceived bad influences in society, so they began to react by methods such as boycotting, advocating restrictive legislation (e.g., antigay, antiabortion, limits on pornography, etc.), or even performing terrorism in extreme cases. This is happening in many places around the world. Marty discusses attempts at religious pluralism or multiculturalism that try to incorporate the stranger, but this in some cases has not worked out as hoped; witness Muslims in Europe, for example. The struggle goes on regarding how to deal with the challenge. In *Collision of Faiths*, Marty raises the key question about the three monotheistic religious traditions: "Can Judaism, Christianity, and Islam be pluralistic? The question is not whether they can tolerate each other, but whether they can accept the idea that other religions have intrinsic religious value even if those values and ways of life contradict in some ways your religion's values and ways of life?" That question is still to be answered.

A Hasidic Jew, David Yerushalmi, who is leading a national effort to enact anti-Sharia legislation, has teamed up with fundamentalist Christians in state legislatures to push what is perceived as anti-Islam legislation. Yerushalmi is reported to have a history of controversial statements about race, immigration, and Islam. Last fall, Oklahoma overwhelmingly approved a constitutional amendment that bans the use of Islamic law, and Tennessee, among other states, is considering such legislation. This is a nonissue being used to stoke anti-immigrant, antireligious sentiments of fundamentalists against perceived enemies in other religions. Author Amy Sullivan says in regard to the Sharia scare tactic:"If you are not vitally concerned about the possibility of radical Muslims infiltrating the U.S. government and establishing a Taliban-style theocracy, then you are not a candidate for the GOP presidential nomination."[58] Then presidential candidate Newt Gingrich jumped on the bandwagon regarding the threat of Sharia law; he just couldn't resist the temptation to denigrate Muslims as an appeal to the base of the party. Another recent shameful attack on American Muslins came from the Florida Family Association. They went after sponsors of the TV show *All-American Muslim* because it does not portray Muslims as radicals. Lowe's was the first company to publicly acknowledge that it had pulled sponsorship from the show, and this precipitated some boycotts of their stores.

On the positive side, Marty's book goes on to mention a great example of pluralism around immigration to New York City (NYC) in the period of rapid influx in the 1800s to early 1900s when so many nationalities and religions arrived in the great melting pot of NYC (Irish Catholics, Protestants, Jews from around the world, etc). Although there was some friction as wave after wave of new immigrant populations arrived, for the most part there was a tolerance and gradual acceptance of the melting pot, which is America's strength. We should not forget this in our time when anti-immigrant, anti-Muslim policies are emerging in different states. Marty concludes that faiths will continue to collide, but individuals and groups that risk hospitality and promote engagement with the stranger will contribute to a world in which measured hopes can survive and those who hope can guide.[59]

Diana Eck undertook the Pluralism Project at Harvard University beginning in1991 and in 2002 published the book *A New Religious America: How a "Christian Country" Has Become the World's Most Religiously Diverse Nation* around the results of that project. The project involved visits and interviews with the immigrants of other faiths. In her book, she describes the impact of the Immigration and Nationality Act of 1965, which dramatically opened up immigration to those around the world. Eck says that although there has been much focus on the topic of immigrants in recent decades, there has not been as much discussion about the religious traditions they brought with them from around the world. Although we have always had a diversity of religions in America, Eck says that the diversity of our religious life has increased dramatically, exponentially.[60] I suspect part of the rising of the fundamentalist religious movement discussed in this section is in reaction to this nearly four decades of rapid immigration from around the world. There has been an effort by the fundamentalists to demonstrate publicly that this is a Christian nation, e.g. placing Christmas displays and the Ten Commandments in public spaces. The not so subtle message to immigrants of other faiths is that you are not true Americans.

Former Bush administration official David Kuo, author of *Tempting Faith: An Inside Story of Political Seduction* writes that Falwell has shaped the image of Jesus for much of America today; unfortunately, his image does not do justice to the Jesus of the gospels. He says: "When people hear 'Christian', too often they think not of Jesus and his teaching but of Jerry Falwell and his politics and it is a turnoff for many."[61] The so-called Moral Majority has now morphed into fundamentalist groupings that believe in literal translation of the Bible and eschew modernity and secular trends; it has become an Evangelical movement that is somewhat split between a more fundamentalist leaning and those who are often more enlightened on issues such as the environment and social justice. Most of these groups tend to be Republican and many have associated with the Tea Party. Although claiming to represent family and moral values, their two overriding issues have been abortion and homosexuality. These are peripheral issues from a Biblical context of a moral life. They miss the central emphasis of justice and compassion in the gospels. It is difficult to see how these "family values" religious groups identify with conservative politicians who are usually pro-war, pro-rich, pro-American to exclusion of others, eschew social justice as preached by the great prophets, and cozy up to big business, which often acts counter to family values interests. Further, they claim to be pro-life, yet their interest seems to wane for children beyond the womb when these so called pro-life Christians embrace right-wing politicians who want to cut child nutrition programs, the Head Start program, health care for children, and the like.

Ironically, it is in the so-called Red states (including much of the Bible Belt region) where one finds earlier child bearing, higher divorce rates, lower education levels, and lower family incomes than the Blue states, which are dominated by more metropolitan coastal states. The set of moral policies that restrict youth sex education largely to abstinence-only programs; condemn cohabitation before marriage; and rail against same-sex unions, marriages, and childrearing; often produce exactly the opposite of what they are intended to do. It amazes me that the political activism of the Religious Right, including the support of right-wing politicians, in recent decades has largely gone against their own moral and economic interests, as I will try to show.

In his *National Journal* article title of May 2010, "Do 'Family Values' Weaken Families?", Jonathan Rauch raises a provocative question. He makes the case that the most stable families are in the areas the Religious Right loves to hate, the so-called elite metropolitan coastal areas.[62] The country's lowest divorce rate belongs to Massachusetts, a liberal coastal Blue state and the first to allow same-sex marriage. The states with the highest divorce rates are predominantly those Red states with the highest percentage of the Religious Right. Naomi Cahn and June Carbone of George Washington University and the University of Missouri (Kansas City), respectively, suggest in their recent book *Red Families vs. Blue families: Legal Polarizations and the Creation of Culture* that this results from a cultural divide that has opened wide over the last few decades. Cahn and Carbone contend that the most important factor in stable marriages is waiting until you are an adult to marry and have children.[63] This has also resulted in higher incomes as a benefit of delayed marriage and childbearing to get higher education.

Cahn and Carbone say that, first and foremost, later marriage is better; adults make better family life decisions. Recent data shows that a majority of mothers under thirty now have children out of wedlock. Yet the Religious Right fights against sex education except for abstinence-only policies. You can guess the result: many early marriages or single motherhood (think of Bristol Palin, whose mother is a big abstinence-education advocate). These youngsters may not have finished high school, very likely won't get higher education, and in many ways are not prepared for raising families. These kids often get into early marriage as the only religiously sanctioned way to initiate sex or through shotgun weddings. Cahn and Carbon's data show that the states with the earliest marriage age are all Red states (Arkansas, Idaho, Kansas, Oklahoma, and Utah), while states with the highest first-marriage age are Blue (Connecticut, Massachusetts, New Jersey, New York, and Rhode Island). The same is true of age of a parent's first childbirth; Massachusetts is highest (about twenty-eight years) and Mississippi lowest (about twenty-three years). A fact of life, say Cahn and Carbone, is that even the most devout are unlikely to make it through higher education degrees without having sex. Ironically, it is the tolerance of urban lifestyles with greater access to birth control and acceptance of cohabitation before marriage that fosters later and more stable marriages. The Blue state metropolitan regions tend to have access to relatively better education, including sex education; later marriage, which often means cohabitation while pursuing higher education; acceptance of homosexual unions and marriage, and so forth. The other interesting thing about higher education is the fact that these women have fewer abortions, exactly the outcome the Religious Right would want to see. And finally, in more affluent Blue state metropolitan regions, families are prospering with two higher-educated professionals heading households. Political commentator Ruth Marcus writes that in 1960, the most- and least-educated adults were equally likely to be married. Now, nearly two-thirds of college graduates are married, compared with less than half of those with a high school diploma or less. Those with less education are less likely to ever marry and more likely to divorce if they do.[64]

So as moral traditionalism fails to stem premarital sex and early childbirth, births precipitate more cases of early marriages and unwed parenthood. This in turn increases family breakdown while reducing education levels and earnings. Yet the response of the Religious Right is to preach more sermons on abstinence-only education and to support political candidates whose policies promote abstinence; they argue for limits on schools providing sex education, they want to legislate against abortions under all circumstances, and they are against gay marriage and childrearing by gay couples. These politicians are also most often those who want to cut government programs, which would likely benefit moderate- to lower-income families in the Religious Right congregations, such as nutrition and school lunch programs, food stamps, Medicaid, Head Start, job training, greater access to education loans, unemployment insurance, and so forth. It's been shown that Red-state populations rely more on government programs because these states are relatively poorer; with lower personal incomes, red-state residents show increased participation in means tested government programs.[65]

And the irony of all this is that the Religious Right wants to push their "family values" on to us Blue state folks; I say no thank you! Seriously, I now better appreciate why the Religious Right talks so much about family values and combating moral breakdown of the family; they are seeing the breakdown every day in and around their Red state congregations. On the other hand, I see little of it in our congregation in Washington DC. We have a large contingent of two-parent families, including many gay and lesbian two-parent families, virtually all of whom married and had children after completing advanced education. They represent the successful poster parents and families for the Cahn and Carbone study. So why would we possibly want to buy into the negative, judgmental family values of the Religious Right, which aren't working anyway? The really sad aspect of all this is that the Religious Right's policies, fed by the like of Rick

Santorum, who promote the combination of bad social policies (like fighting contraception and family planning) and espouse negative views of higher education, will only lead to a worsening economic inequality gap between metropolitan oriented Blue states and more rural Red states.

The issue of contraception has gotten completely out of hand in this presidential primary season of 2012. We see old white men on the campaign trail, in Congressional hearings, among state legislatures, and among Catholic Bishops trying to impose their 1950s beliefs against contraception (one legislator even suggested that women might try the contraception method of the 1950s when, he said, women should put an aspirin between their legs as a birth control measure!). Evangelical pastors recently endorsed Rick Santorum as their preferred Republican presidential candidate. This seems to relate to the fact that Santorum is the most up-front about wanting the government to regulate people's sexual and reproductive habits. A *Washington Monthly* blog reports that Santorum actually said during the current campaign, "One of the things I will talk about, that no president has talked about before, is I think the dangers of contraception in this country....It's not okay. It's a license to do things in a sexual realm that is counter to how things are supposed to be."[66] At the same time, the Center for Disease Control reports that 99 percent of American women use birth control during their reproductive lifetime. To prevent unwanted pregnancies and abortions through family planning would seem to be a desirable outcome for even religious and political conservatives. And it's an economic issue as well; for millions of American women, their economic and physical well-being is determined by when and if they get pregnant. Recent analysis shows that women are becoming the primary or senior breadwinner in many families.[67] This advancement for women in higher education and in the workforce has largely been made possible by family planning (with contraception), which allows women to delay childbearing until completing advanced education and getting established in the workplace. Yet, many of the presidential candidates were actively campaigning against family planning funding, particularly former candidate Rick Santorum and his wife, who are apparently among the 1 percent who choose not to use contraception. So, again we have the 1 percent trying to overwhelm the 99 percent. Sadly, many Conservative state legislators and governors are cutting back family planning under the guise of deficit control. For example, in Texas, the Religious and Political Right are taking their war against Planned Parenthood to the point where clinics serving poor women are being forced to close for lack of state funds. The result will almost surely be more abortions. Why does the Right always seem compelled to act against its own interests?

I was glad to see that leaders of mainline Christian, Jewish, and Muslim national organizations affirmed support for women's rights to make decisions about their sexual and reproductive health without government restrictions on their access to health care options. They said: "We stand with President Obama and Secretary Sebelius in their decision to reaffirm the importance of contraceptive services as essential preventive care for women under the Patient Protection and Affordable Care Act, and to assure access under the law to American women, regardless of religious affiliation. We respect individuals' moral agency to make decisions about their sexuality and reproductive health without governmental interference or legal restrictions. We do not believe that specific religious doctrine belongs in health care reform – as we value our nation's commitment to church-state separation. We believe that women and men have the right to decide whether or not to apply the principles of their faith to family planning decisions, and to do so they must have access to (health) services."[68]

It is sad to see these counterproductive social and economic policies being promoted by those who claim to be the most religious among us. In regard to family values, my Judeo-Christian heritage teaches love, support, and nourishment of family and community, not the divisiveness I sense from the Religious Right. Beyond that basic foundation, my family values tend toward later marriages; they include the provision of good sex education and acceptance of cohabitation before marriage, which in turn tends to foster higher education and job security before marriage; and finally, my family values also include respect for gay unions, marriage, and childrearing. These are all values that are pretty widely accepted in my religious tradition and my

41

congregation at Luther Place, yet it is these policies that are roundly criticized as liberal, elitist, urban secularism and socialism by the Religious Right. I think that across much of the political and religious spectrum, we can agree that abortion should be a last resort and that two-parent families (including gay parents) are the preferred model where possible (hardliners within the Religious Right would insist that abortion is never an option and flatly oppose gay parenting). Why can't the rest of us work together to try to encourage such pro-family policies?

Cox sees the fundamentalist Christian movement in the United States in decline because of their extremes and because of the changing demographics of the country. But the movement seems to be making a last gasp to try to influence social trends they don't like. For example, North Carolina, a state that already bans gay marriage, recently went further by passing a constitutional amendment which seals the door on same-sex marriages but also apparently voids other types of domestic unions. The Rev. Billy Graham and other evangelical leaders along with conservative legislators led the way on this initiative.[69] Of course, the Evangelical hypocrisy on this issue is well-documented with the infamous cases of evangelical leaders whose homosexual activity has been revealed.[70] As Cox suggests, this may well be an example of the last gasp of fundamentalism trying to close the doors on homosexuals before it is too late as an increasing number of states are expanding gay rights. What will happen to fundamentalism when, as is likely in a few years, gay rights will be widely accepted in the United States and will no longer be a polarizing issue? That leaves them with only women's reproductive matters as a political issue, which seems like a very narrow agenda for a Christian movement. Younger Evangelicals are rejecting the extreme views of many of the Religious Right, particularly in regard to homosexuality. They are also recognizing that the gospel is much more about social justice than the narrow agenda of their leaders. So I expect demographics will work against the Religious Right's narrow social agenda.

In one of the many hypocrisies of our time, religious Fundamentalists held the so-called Values Voter Summit in Washington DC on October

7–8, 2011; they invited the Republican presidential candidates and other Conservative and Fundamentalist voices to speak. Multiple media sources reported some of the extremism on display at the summit; Muslims, gays, and Mormons were particular targets.[71] For example, Robert Jeffress, the senior pastor at First Baptist church in Dallas called Mormonism a cult and said "Mormonism is not Christianity" while he was introducing Romney-rival Rick Perry. It was reported by NPR that when Perry took the stage, his reaction was to say to the crowd: "Didn't Pastor Jeffress hit it out of the park?" So does that mean Perry supports this bigotry?[72]

Christian extremist Bryan Fischer of the American Family Association, who spoke at the summit after candidate Mitt Romney, is reported to have made a passionate case against Sharia law in the United States, called homosexuality, among other things, a "threat to public health," and stated that "we must choose as a nation between homosexuality and liberty, because we cannot have both." He insisted that Muslims and Christians don't worship the same God, and both he and Jeffress are reported to have also said that only a true Christian can serve in the White House. This is the same Bryan Fischer who is reported by *Religion Dispatches* magazine to have argued that the Constitution's First Amendment (freedom of religion) does not apply to non-Christians, including Mormons.[73]

Two participants at the Values Voter Summit had the will to stand up against this bigotry and extremism. It was reported that before presidential candidate Mitt Romney took the podium at the summit, conservative commentator Bill Bennett challenged Jeffress by saying, "Do not give voice to bigotry." And Romney, to his credit, took issue with Fischer when he said during his remarks: "One of the speakers who will follow me today, has crossed that line I think. Poisonous language does not advance our cause. It has never softened a single heart nor changed a single mind. The blessings of faith carry the responsibility of civil and respectful debate." Nevertheless, in a straw poll at this forum, Romney received only 4 percent of the vote; there is clearly a problem among Fundamentalists and Evangelicals with a Mormon (rather than a "true" Christian) candidate for president.[74] If this so-called Values Voters Summit was really about family values, why wouldn't these fundamentalist Christians be supporting strong family-oriented candidates like Mitt Romney or President Obama over the likes of Newt Gingrich (who at the time of the summit was the social conservative favorite in Iowa), who is on his third wife after having so blatantly violated wedding vows to his previous wives. Gingrich's pandering to this group went over the top recently, with his attack on 'activist' judges and his vow to establish a White House commission upon taking office to examine threats to religious freedom in the United States. I suspect the only religious freedoms he is proposing to protect are those of the Religious Right who rail against gay rights, try to prevent reproductive rights of other faithful individuals, and who want to restrict Muslim rights in this country.

During the recent Louisiana Republican primary campaign in March 2012, candidate Rick Santorum visited, applauded, and was blessed by Greenwell Springs Baptist Church Pastor Dennis Terry. In a released movie clip, the evangelical pastor is seen telling the assembled crowd that anyone who doesn't worship God should leave the country, and then called on people to "stand up against" gay people, liberals, and women who have abortions. He is further recorded saying: "Listen to me. If you don't love America, and you don't like the way we do things, I've got one thing to say, get out! … We don't worship Buddha, we don't worship Mohammed, we don't worship Allah. We worship God. We worship God's son Jesus Christ." To rapturous applause, Pastor Terry continued: "As long as they continue to kill little babies in our mother's womb, somebody's got to take a stand and say it's not right. God be merciful to us as a nation. As long as sexual perversion is becoming normalized, somebody needs to stand up and say God forgive us, God have mercy upon us." Santorum was shown clapping approvingly in the background as the right-wing pastor delivered the ranting fire-and-brimstone address. He later received a personal blessing from the preacher, who called on God's will to be done in the upcoming election.[75]

The president of the New Evangelical Partnership for the Common Good, Richard Cizik, challenges the alliance of the Christian fundamentalists with the right wing of the Republican Party, particularly when they advocate abolishing many of the programs that serve "the least of these," which Jesus emphasized in his ministry. He says, "most 'values voters' with even a minimal degree of biblical literacy recognize that the Hebrew prophets and Jesus warned the powerful not to afflict the poor and comfort the rich. These bedrock Judeo-Christian principles are flouted by conservatives who demand cuts to nutrition programs that help low-income women feed their children even as they defend tax loopholes for some of the world's wealthiest people." He thinks it's time for a new values debate about issues such as economic fairness, health care, and immigration by those biblically based religious folks who don't think the religious right speaks for the faith community.[76]

Although Christian fundamentalist and evangelical labels often get used interchangeably, Evangelicals are more diverse and, increasingly among younger Evangelicals, are more social justice oriented. This diversity among Evangelicals is illustrated by John Stott, a gentle British scholar who recently died, who was never a firebrand like Jerry Falwell or Pat Robertson. Instead, he quietly counseled Christians to follow the example of Jesus, especially his concern for the poor and oppressed and for dealing with social ills such as racial oppression.. Richard Cizik, president of the New Evangelical Partnership for the Common Good is quoted as saying: "Against the quackery and anti-intellectualism of our (so-called 'Moral Majority') movement, Stott made it possible to say you are evangelical and not be apologetic." Unfortunately, the Stotts of the world lost out in media attention to Evangelical and fundamentalist Moral Majority leaders like Falwell and Robertson. I personally resonate with evangelicals like John Stott. As a member of the Evangelical Lutheran Church of America (ELCA), I resent that the original meaning of "evangelical" has been hijacked and totally misrepresented by the likes of Falwell and Robertson. At the time of the Reformation, theologians began to embrace the term evangelical as referring to "gospel truth." Martin Luther referred to the "evangelical" church to distinguish Protestants from Catholics in the Roman Catholic Church. Particularly in Scandinavian countries and among Lutherans more widely, the term has continued to be used in a broad sense.[77]

In regard to fundamentalist strains in Judaism, I recently witnessed the growing Orthodox and ultra-Orthodox sects in Israel, many of whom believe they were uniquely given title to the Holy Land by God, support settlement in the West Bank, resist peace initiatives, have large families with six to eight children, and largely cut themselves off from the rest of society. They are also now forcing changes in broader Israeli society, such as limiting women's images in advertising, requiring separation of men and women on buses when serving Orthodox neighborhoods, and restrictions on military women.

The Jerusalem Center for Public Affairs says on their website:"Active fundamentalists among the Jews have largely been confined to those religiously inclined messianists who believe that through a particular set of activities they can hasten the day of redemption. For some, these activities mainly involve religiously settling what they consider the biblical Land of Israel. Having elevated this 'commandment' above nearly all the other 612, they are convinced that by doing so they are being true to the fundamentals of Judaism. There are other active Jewish fundamentalists for whom the redemption can be hastened not by settlements but by acts of Jewish ritual activity. For these fundamentalists, Judaism is boiled down not to the need to establish settlements in the God-promised land but to the practice of a set of ritual acts—lighting Sabbath candles, donning phylacteries, giving charity, and so on—whose performance by all Jews—and in some cases also by non-Jews—will hasten the day of the Messiah's return and hence the redemption. For these active fundamentalists, the world is divided…between those who are joined with them and those who are their opponents. The fact that they see enemies nearby, both from within and without, only encourages them to continue in the struggle and trust that history will vindicate their efforts."[78]

Approximately 5 million of the world's 13 million Jews live in the United States. There are basically three major movements in the United States today: Reform, Conservative, and Orthodox. Haredi Judaism is the most conservative form of Orthodox Judaism, often referred to as ultra-Orthodox. Haredi Jews, like other Orthodox Jews, consider their belief system and religious practices to extend in an unbroken chain back to Moses and the giving of the Torah on Mount Sinai. As a result, they regard non-Orthodox, and to an extent Modern Orthodox, streams of Judaism to be deviations from authentic Judaism. The United States is home to the second-largest Haredi population; the sect represents about 10 percent of U.S. Judaism.[79] For the most part, there have not been politically activist or violent strains within fundamentalist Judaism in the United States. An exception that I noted earlier is a fundamentalist Hasidic Jew, David Yerushalmi, who is leading a national effort to enact anti-Sharia legislation around the country, thus stoking anti-Muslim sentiments that have already risen because of 9/11 and subsequent Islamic terrorism in various parts of the world.

These fundamentalist trends in religion that have emerged in recent decades are a concern worldwide, as they try to turn back the clock to earlier times when women and minorities were put in their subservient place. In the following section, I will discuss more progressive movements in society and religion that are working for justice for all.

3

Emerging Progressive Trends Spurred by the Faithful and Spiritual

Religious Diversity in the United States

Before talking specifically about progressive trends in religion and society, I want to treat the subject of religious diversity in America.

Diana Eck's Pluralism Project, mentioned earlier, involved visits and interviews with immigrants of other faiths. The results of the project show that, without doubt, we are now the most religiously diverse nation in the world. Eck paints a picture of the religious diversity in various communities around the United States. She says that Los Angeles is the most complex Buddhist city in the world, with a Buddhist population spanning the whole range of the Asian Buddhist world from Sri Lanka to Korea, along with a multitude of native-born American Buddhists. She also mentions the Washington DC suburbs where I live. Along New Hampshire Avenue in Montgomery County, Maryland, there is a new Cambodian Buddhist temple, then a Muslim community center set between an onion-domed Ukrainian Orthodox Church and a Disciples of Christ church. Farther along is a Gujarati Hindu temple, and just off New Hampshire Avenue are a Jain temple and a range of churches sharing space, with Hispanic Pentecostal,

Vietnamese Catholic, and Korean evangelical congregations among others. Eck cites many other examples of diverse religious communities around the country. Although we have had a few politically motivated examples of trying to prevent mosques from being built, for the most part America absorbs this diversity and benefits from it; the United States is still the great melting pot of the world.[80]

In his book *America and the Challenges of Religious Diversity*, Robert Wuthnow provides a comprehensive review of religious pluralism based on an extensive religion and diversity survey his team completed. He says: "By the end of the twentieth century, Americans were well prepared in one sense to accommodate the wider range of religious diversity that was rapidly becoming a reality. Yet in another sense the new religious diversity posed a challenge that would not so easily be met. This was the challenge of having to rethink the presumption that America itself was basically Christian (or Judeo-Christian) as had been the historic view. These new questions cannot easily be glossed over by embracing multiculturalism." [81] Witness what is happening in Europe, where Prime Minister Cameron of Great Britain has called multiculturalism a failure. This reaction stems at least in part from the domestically bred Islamic terrorist sympathizers who have emerged in several European countries.

Although Wuthnow says the share of Muslim, Hindu, or Buddhist is quite small, the impact of these groups on American culture is much larger. Millions of Americans who are Christians or Jews come in contact with persons of these minority religions at work and in their communities. Millions have visited mosques and temples or traveled to countries in which non-Western religions are predominant, yet their responses are quite varied. Although it is easy to give lip service to the value of diversity, many Americans still say that they would not welcome these religions becoming a bigger presence in our society.

From the viewpoint of other religions, Wuthnow found that American Hindus, Buddhists, and Muslims are keenly aware that theirs are minority religions in the United States. The experience of living among Christians by members of these religions is quite varied. Many have faced some form of discrimination but overall say that living in the United States has been good; they argue that the nation's laws and customs provide desired freedom and opportunity. In fact, Wuthnow says, a recent Gallup survey showed that Muslims are particularly optimistic about the future in the United States despite some of the anti-Muslin language that emerged after 9/11.

Not included in the discussion above is the view of Mormonism. A poll by Pew Research in 2008 found that white, evangelical Protestants are more uncomfortable with the idea of a Mormon presidential candidate than are other Republicans and Independents. This was exemplified at the Values Voter Summit in Washington D.C. in the fall of 2011, when prominent evangelical leader Robert Jeffress told reporters that Mormonism was a cult and that Romney was not a Christian. Jeffress, whose church is a prominent member of the Southern Baptist Convention, began making his point during the introduction: "Do we want a candidate who is a good moral person, or do we want a candidate who is a born-again follower of Jesus Christ? In Rick Perry, we have a candidate who is a committed follower of Christ."[82] On the other hand, the Mormon Church has certain practices that alienate other faiths. One example is that despite a 1995 agreement by the Mormon Church to stop baptizing dead Jews by proxy, it was discovered recently that Anne Frank, teenage writer killed during the Holocaust, was baptized by proxy by the Mormon Church in February of 2012.[83]

Wuthnow, based on the analysis of the religion and diversity survey his team conducted, breaks down the contemporary faithful responses into three groups, which he calls spiritual shopping, Christian inclusivism, and Christian exclusivism. Obviously all respondents don't neatly fit into these categories, but it helps clarify broad differences among the faithful in the United States.

1. He describes the spiritual shopping group as making choices and having the freedom to choose according to one's personal tastes and needs. Some may have experimented with Eastern religions, but for most it has not resulted in joining the minority religions but rather in giving a new outlook on what it means to be a religious person.

2. The second group is Christian inclusivism. They are the churchgoers, the large majority of Americans who faithfully adhere to some or many of traditional teachings and practices, but who accept religious diversity.

3. The final group, called Christian exclusivism, has a much more closed view of religious practice. Wuthnow says "These Americans firmly defend what they regard as an old-fashioned, exclusivist version of the gospel truth." They believe that only their Christian group is saved and going to heaven, and they believe in trying to convert nonbelievers and people of other faiths.

In the survey, 31 percent of the American public qualified as spiritual shoppers according to the criteria chosen, Christian inclusivists made up 23 percent, and Christian exclusivists 34 percent; another 11 percent didn't fit neatly into one of these categories. When the respondents were asked whether Christianity is the only way to have a true personal relationship with God, only 5 percent of spiritual shoppers agreed; 62 and 78 percent of inclusivists and exclusivists agreed, respectively. The difference between the spiritual shoppers and the other two groups is pretty dramatic and would seem to be a challenge for interreligious dialogue. When asked whether the United States was founded on Christian principles, 30 percent of spiritual shoppers said yes, while 55 percent of inclusivists and 68 percent of exclusivists said yes. As I move forward to the next section of my book, I would expect the audience for progressive social justice ideas I discuss to be from among the 53 percent of faithful who were identified as spiritual shoppers or Christian inclusivists in Wuthnow's analysis, although there is an increasing segment of Evangelicals who would normally identify with the exclusivists but who have become more social justice oriented. For example, Bob Edgar, in his book *Middle Church*, describes a letter sent in 2005 to then President George W. Bush from Evangelicals for Social Action calling on the president to put increased emphasis on reducing hunger and poverty here and abroad. They made the point that faith-based agencies cannot by themselves solve problems of poverty. They went on to say: "We believe our rich nation should agree that everyone who works full time responsibly will be able to earn enough to rise above the poverty level and enjoy health insurance..." This illustrates the importance of not stereotyping Evangelicals. Many are potential partners in collaborative social justice initiatives.[84]

Emerging Progressive/Spirituality Movements in Religion

Jim Wallis of Sojourners, in his book *The Great Awakening*, says that there is a revival of faith happening worldwide, and that historically such revivals, or Great Awakenings as he calls them, have changed social and political circumstances as well. He says "In the churches, a combination of deeper compassion and better theology has moved many far beyond the partisan politics of the religious right." There is also a growing spiritual movement that is largely outside the institutional church. One of the key challenges going forward is how to tap the power of these multiple progressive movements in a coordinated fashion to address the many social justice issues of our day.

In her book *Christianity for the Rest of Us*, Diana Butler Bass reports on a new vitality and transformation going on in a significant number of mainline Protestant congregations, unlike the prevailing impression that mainline churches are dying institutions. She says about these so-called transformational congregations: "Typically they have rediscovered the riches of the Christian past and practice simple, but profound, things such as discernment, hospitality, testimony, contemplation, and justice...They focus more on God's grace than on the eternal state of their own souls."

She describes a religious transformation that is going on, particularly among younger adults.

I think there's a shift away from entertainment-oriented, program-based megachurches among younger adults to wanting to be part of a genuine spiritual community where they can learn a tradition, school their children in tradition, as they're now getting married and having young families, and where they can connect with other people in community who are the same age and who are interested in some of the same things they're interested in.

She goes on to say,

The people in the mainline congregations I'm studying are as dissatisfied with their bureaucratic and denominational structures as these emerging evangelicals are with the traditional patterns of setting up evangelical congregations. On both sides of this conversation, they're reaching toward new kinds of structures. [85]

As exciting as this transformational trend is within mainline churches, there are clearly many who have become disenchanted with the institutional church. Author Phyllis Tickle, in her book, *The Great Emergence,* goes so far as to suggest we are seeing religious change on the scale of the Great Reformation. She quotes an Anglican Bishop, Mark Dyer, who humorously says that every five hundred years the Church feels compelled to hold a giant rummage sale and that we are living through one of those periods now. She postulates that it started around the Civil War issue of slavery. Both sides claimed biblical authority in their arguments about slavery. The bible does not support slavery, but it acknowledges the practice in ancient society and does not specifically condemn it. So supporters of slavery were able to cite selected passages that appeared to condone slavery while abolitionists like Harriet Beecher Stowe argued that the overall justice message of the bible should prevail. Tickle suggests that the issue of slavery was a turning point for Protestantism in regard to Martin Luther's reformation doctrine of 'sola scriptura' (i.e., authority comes from scripture alone). The slavery issue caused a split in the Church and major questioning of the authority of scripture. She goes on to cite the role of women in society and the church and sexual orientation as other key issues that challenge rigid views of biblical authority in recent times. These issues and more are causing a significant churning within the Church. Tickle goes on to say that when such upheaval happens we usually see two new forms of religion emerge. Five hundred years ago, Protestantism emerged along with a reformed Catholic Church. So today, we see new forms of Christianity emerging but we are also witnessing transformation within the mainline churches as described by Diana Butler Bass earlier.

Two of the key movements of recent decades to develop outside the traditional church are the emerging church movement and New Monasticism which I discuss in the following paragraphs.

The emerging church movement, a Christian movement that crosses a number of theological boundaries first emerged in the U.K. and spread to the United States and other nations. Movement leaders claim that it transcends labels such as conservative and liberal. They typically speak of their disillusionment with the organized and institutional church. In an article "The Emerging Church Movement and Young Adults," by Gerardo Marti of Davidson College, the author says:

> Overall, the Emerging Church Movement attempts to rescue core aspects of Christianity from the entanglement of modernity, bureaucracy, and right-wing politics. For example, organizationally, today's Christianity is viewed as burdened with CEO-styled pastors, excessive concern for organizational maintenance with routinized, predictable, yet culturally-irrelevant ministry practices. Slick, mall-styled megachurches with five-point sermons and large carbon-footprint campuses are targets for criticism. On an individual level, Christianity is seen as overly concerned with simplistic views of gaining salvation, oppressive anxieties about personal morality, judgmental stances toward other religious commitments, and apathy toward social justice issues like gender equity, race relations, and environmentalism.[86]

Perhaps the most comprehensive treatment of the emerging church movement is by Gibbs and Bolger in their book *Emerging Churches: Creating Christian Community in Postmodern Cultures*. Gibbs and Bolger interviewed over one hundred people involved in leading emerging churches, and from this research they have identified some core values in the emerging church, including desires to imitate the life of Jesus, transform secular society, emphasize communal living, welcome outsiders, be generous and creative, and lead without control. They contend that the church must embody the gospel within the culture of postmodernity for the Western church to survive the twenty-first century; nineteenth century (or older) tradition will not adequately speak to twenty-first century culture. They also contend that no one knows at this point what a postmodern or a post-Christendom expression of faith look like; it is still taking shape. Much of the emerging church momentum has been with Generation X (Gen X) and to some extent Millenials, who don't see the baby boomer generation's suburban churches as meeting their needs.

Gibbs and Bolger describe nine practices common to these innovative church movements. The first three are core practices for all emerging communities. Most emerging churches also include some mix of the other six practices list below:

1. Identifying with the life of Jesus (rather than specific beliefs or doctrines)
2. Transforming secular space (removing barriers between sacred and secular spaces)
3. Living as community (modeling Jesus and the early church)
4. Welcoming the stranger (modeling Jesus and his ministry to the dispossessed)
5. Serving with generosity (again modeling Jesus and the early church community)
6. Participating as producers (changing from passive to active participation in worship)
7. Creating as created beings (all in community use their creative abilities)
8. Leading as a body (group leadership vs. traditional, pastor-focused model)

9. Taking part in spiritual activities (very important to emerging churches both corporately and individually)

The first core practice, indentifying with the life of Jesus, is most central. To many, the institutional church seems to be missing the centrality of Jesus' message in the Gospels. Emerging churches look more at the pre-Easter Jesus and his teaching and way of life with his disciples rather than focusing on doctrine that has been laid on by the institutional church through the ages. The gospel is viewed as an invitation to a new way of life on earth rather than a belief in some abstract doctrine oriented to qualifying for heaven. Our mission in the here and now is the emphasis. Some new communities begin with the Sermon on the Mount and the Beatitudes. What a great place to start; it leaves no doubt in the community's mind as to the focus of Jesus' message. Gibbs and Bolger say, "Jesus created an alternative social order, one built on servanthood and forgiveness, through the activities he performed as a leader of a counter-temple movement." Jesus' vision of the Kingdom of God was different then the religious hierarchy in control of the temple. Many in the emerging church see their mission as counter institutional to the church hierarchies of our time. They also fully recognize the different place and time of the Gospels and are able to put Jesus' message in the context of our postmodern times; literal interpretations of scripture simply do not work for the postmodern culture.

The second core practice according to Gibbs and Bolger is transforming secular space. It implies no separation of secular and sacred spaces. Rather than a Sunday focus on the sacred in a defined church building and the remainder of the week focused on secular matters, emerging churches seek God's Kingdom in their everyday lives. The focus is on a 24-7 way of life.

The third core practice is living as community. Emerging churches have a strong emphasis on community rather than an individualistic, salvation-oriented approach to Christianity. Emerging churches tend to be either small groups or networks of small groups focused on coming together in community. They periodically come together as a whole, some on the traditional Sunday gathering day, some on a monthly basis, but many others only as needed. The small groups in community are the primary focus, with meetings of the whole as a secondary priority. The attempt is to model Jesus and the early church communities.

Emerging communities also include many, but not necessarily all, of the remaining six practices. They are welcoming communities that stress the value of caring for one another; quite a number also participate in social justice projects in their neighborhoods. The communities usually do not have structured leadership, and there is clearly much more active participation by the whole community in worship experiences as compared to traditional churches. The communities also tend to be more spiritual oriented then traditional churches and include much more of the arts. [87]

In any case, below are two examples of emerging churches that are mentioned in the Gibbs and Bolger study:

1. Church of the Apostles, in Seattle, which is affiliated with both the Lutheran and Episcopalian churches, is a bit unusual since it is associated, albeit loosely, with the institutional church. The community is an example of the diversity of worship and music styles in emerging communities, often a blending of ancient liturgy styles with postmodern styles. Former Pastor Karen Ward says "Some people 'can't get to the theology' by singing 16th-century German hymns, others don't find enough of a sense of awe and mystery in contemporary-style church services. The community tries to combine the best of both worlds in their services, held Saturdays at 5 p.m. at St. John Lutheran Church in Phinney Ridge. They use ancient liturgies and Bible readings, along with a live band. They'll mix rock music and opera music sometimes. Ward calls it a postmodern, or 'ancient/future' approach using "everything the church has is in the treasure chest that we can use" Ultimately, Ward says, emerging churches are about asking: "What was it that caused the church to grow in the early days? I think it was the authenticity of the way of life. It wasn't an institution at all then. It was people following in the path of Jesus' way of life.

It's about getting back to the core of Christianity, but in a way that's accessible to today's postmodern world."[88]

2. House of Mercy, St. Paul: Debbie Blue relates (in Gibbs and Bolger's book) coming from a very conservative Baptist church background, attending Yale for a couple years, then taking an internship with the Lutheran Campus Center in Madison, Wisconsin; she worked there and for two big Lutheran Churches. After that experience, she decided that she probably couldn't work for the institutional church. She and her husband and another pastor friend moved to the Minneapolis area and decided to start a new church. Pastor Blue wrote recently in an article for *Sojourners* magazine about House of Mercy, particularly highlighting its diversity. She describes the congregants as "old and young, from Catholic, mainline, fundamentalist, and atheist backgrounds, gay, straight, working class, intellectual, Buddhist, Quaker, drunks, in recovery, artists, and musicians. They are square, circular, zigzag, hyphenated, and occasionally Republican."[89] There is also a House of Mercy band, an alt-country group operating out of the church, which plays at other venues such as the St. Paul Turf Club.[90]

New Monasticism seems to be the latest version of the emerging church but with somewhat different practices. Christianity Today reports that "a June 2004 conference officially marks the birth of the new monasticism, and participants wrote a voluntary rule for the many and diverse communities. New communities and academics met in Durham, North Carolina, with older communities like the Mennonite Reba Place Fellowship, Bruderhof, and the Catholic Worker. Drawing from church tradition and borrowing the term *new monasticism* from Jonathan R. Wilson's book *Living Faithfully in a Fragmented World* (Morehouse, 1998), participants developed 12 distinctives that would mark these communities, including: submission to the larger church, living with the poor and outcast, living near community members, hospitality, nurturing a common community life and a shared economy, peacemaking, reconciliation, care for creation, celibacy or monogamous marriage, formation of new members along the lines of the old novitiate, and contemplation."[91]

New monastic communities have also been bubbling up in the UK for some time and are now developing in most all the mainline denominations. New monastic communities are also reported in Germany, Holland, Canada, India, New Zealand, Australia, South America, and the Philippines."[92]

Two U.S. examples of new monastic communities include:

1. The Simple Way. Author Shane Claiborne (*The Irresistible Revolution*) is one of the founding members of the Simple Way religious community in Philadelphia, Pennsylvania. This community, which began modestly in a house with six residents in 1998, was featured on the cover of *Christianity Today* as a pioneer in the new monasticism movement. Simple Way is located in a poor neighborhood called Kensington, where the community provides various services to residents of the area. They try to emulate early Christians who came together in community and shared what they had with all those in the community.

2. New Day monastic community in Dallas includes four houses of intentional Christian community centered on rhythms of prayer and mission. The diverse community eats supper together, worships, and shares Holy Communion. Half the members are refugees from countries in Africa; the rest are students, mostly from Perkins School of Theology. About twenty Perkins students receive one-year scholarships to live in the houses, experience monastic life deeply, and gain understanding of God sending the church into the world to witness to and participate in Christ's work.[93] Dr. Elaine Heath, who is at Perkins and connected with New Day, has coauthored a book called *Longing for Spring: A New Vision for Wesleyan Community,* in which Heath and Kisker challenge the church, both within and beyond Wesleyan traditions, to consider the possibility of revitalizing the church through the new monasticism.

The emerging church movements don't fit neatly into any label on the liberal to conservative spectrum or demographic group, but they do tend to reject rigid doctrines and institutions, accept universal religious concepts, and tend toward progressive environmental and social justice policies. Many people in the movement express concern for assuring God's kingdom on earth, by which they mean social justice.

The emerging church movement, in particular, seems to be in a transition and maturing process (some have even suggested it is dying), and the outcome is still to be determined. Phyllis Tickle predicts that by the time the "Great Emergence" matures, it could include a majority of practicing American Christians. Two other authors I discuss later, Harvey Cox and Matthew Fox, also talk in terms of a new reformation or transformation of Christianity. Both Fox and Tickle talk about the parallels to the Great Reformation and somewhat equate the revolutionary forces of change now, such as the Internet and rapid advancement of scientific knowledge, with the Reformation period that saw the emergence of the printing press and early scientific knowledge from Copernicus and others. Change is definitively in the air, but I think it's a bit too early to know what will emerge from all this churning.

The above discussion about the "Great Emergence" does not particularly focus on demographics, however, I would be remiss in not looking at the emerging demographics of our nation and the potential influence the latest generation could have on the progressive agenda. The emerging churches have been heavily populated by members of Generation X (Gen X) who tend to shop for meaningful faith experiences much more than their boomer parents, who generally stayed in the same religion they were born into. The emerging Millennial generation is more of an open question in regard to faith and their role in the emerging church movement. A Center for American Progress report, "New Progressive America: The Millennial Generation" highlights the diversity and progressive attitudes of this generation born between 1978 and 2000. The report shows how this group is increasingly emerging as a progressive voting bloc, including a description of its positive impact on the Obama election in 2008.

The report goes on to say: "One likely consequence of the Millennial generation's rise is an end to the so-called culture wars that have marked American politics for the last several decades. Acrimonious disputes about family and religious values, feminism, gay rights, and race have frequently crippled progressives' ability to make their case to the average American. Millennials support gay marriage, take race and gender equality as givens, are tolerant of religious and family diversity, have an open and positive attitude toward immigration, and generally display little interest in fighting over the divisive social issues of the past. Almost two-thirds agree that religious faith should focus more on promoting tolerance, social justice, and peace in society, and less on opposing abortion or gay rights."[94] The report concludes "We are on course for a new progressive America, and the rise of the Millennial generation is one main force behind this transformation." In regard to religion, they describe the Millennial group as much more spiritual than religious and less affiliated with traditional organized religions than previous generations.[95] Similar to members of Gen X, their indifference to the institutional church will be a challenge for faith-based progressives in forming alliances for social action.

All in all, the analysis in this section suggests there is a more progressive view about social issues among post–baby boomers, including among evangelical youth, but there is also a move in this age group away from the institutional church. The challenging path forward would see progressive mainline churches jointly advocating for justice with emerging church and new monastic communities as well as with spiritual progressives who are not actively involved with a faith community. Current religious organizations promoting social justice will have to adapt to this changing environment.

Progressive Nonprofits That Bring Together Spiritual and Religious Members to Action for The Common Good

As discussed throughout this book, progressive social and political action is needed today more than ever. This section reviews a sampling of the many nonprofit, faith-oriented organizations that advocate for justice in our society.

Sojourners, based in Washington DC, sets a good example of how to conduct faith-based social and political action. Their mission is to articulate the biblical call to social justice, inspiring hope and building a movement to transform individuals, communities, the church, and the world. Recent action included mobilization of national religious leaders around budget deficit issues. The group says that: "Budgets are moral documents, and how we reduce future deficits are historic and defining moral choices. As Christian leaders, we urge Congress and the administration to give moral priority to programs that protect the life and dignity of poor and vulnerable people in these difficult times, our broken economy, and our wounded world. It is the vocation and obligation of the church to speak and act on behalf of those Jesus called 'the least of these."[96]

Sojourners is also a leader in developing interfaith coalitions for political action on behalf of justice. An example is the interfaith Circle of Protection mentioned earlier. National faith leaders representing the Circle of Protection recently met with President Obama and senior White House staff members to urge protection for programs affecting the most vulnerable in society during the debt crisis negotiations. Jim Wallis of Sojourners reported that "We told the president about how a 'Circle of Protection' has formed in response to this crisis. It is now the most unified and broadest coalition of churches that any of us has ever seen—and is endorsed by our brothers and sisters of other faiths and secular organizations who also work for low-income people. In an engaging back and forth conversation, the president and faith leaders discussed how we can get our fiscal house in order without doing so on the backs of those who are most vulnerable. We shared the concern that the deficit must be cut in a way that protects the safety net, and struggling families and children, and maintains our national investments in the future of all of us."[97] Faith in Public Life (FPL) is a communications and organizing resource center dedicated to helping faith leaders reclaim the values debate in America for justice, compassion, and the common good. FPL's website, www.faithinpubliclife.org, is a valuable resource to activists, faith leaders, and journalists, with an active blog and daily news clips from media outlets around the country. Faithful America (affiliated with FPL) describes itself as:"an online community of tens of thousands of citizens motivated by faith to take action on the pressing moral issues." Faithful America was previously hosted by the National Council of Churches in Christ (NCCC). In August 2007, Faith in Public Life became host of Faithful America.

The Network of Spiritual Progressives (NSP) grew out of a Jewish tradition of tikkun olam (healing the world); its lead founder was Rabbi Michael Lerner, also founder of *Tikkun* magazine. Their website indicates that NSP believes that a serious commitment to God, religion, and spirit should manifest in social activism aimed at peace, universal disarmament, social justice with a preferential option for the needs of the poor and oppressed, a commitment to end poverty, hunger, homelessness, inadequate education, and inadequate health care. The NSP welcomes secular humanists, atheists and people who are "spiritual but not religious," as well as people from every religious community who share the values of love, generosity, creativity, wonder and a commitment to respect one another.[98]

The New Evangelical Partnership for the Common Good (NEP) is an evangelical-based organization that promotes social justice based on the teachings of Jesus. Their social justice orientation offers an important opportunity for collaboration from more progressive religious based communities like FPL and NSP who are seeking many of the same objectives. The following are important principles, issues, and causes NEP lists on its website:

- We stand against human degradation and for the human rights of all people, especially the rights of the most vulnerable and despised.
- We stand against war and for peacemaking. We are committed to peacemaking efforts between the world's major religious traditions and especially in the Middle East, where tensions remain high.
- We stand against the devaluing of human life and for a society in which no woman feels that abortion is her only choice.
- We stand against environmental denialism and for God's endangered creation.

- We stand against needless human suffering due to lack of health care and for human health. We stand against the collapse of marriage and for stronger family life. (Note: NEP goes on to say that they do not believe that denigrating the dignity and denying the human rights of gays and lesbians is a legitimate part of a "pro-family" Christian agenda, and will work to reform Christian attitudes and treatment of lesbian and gay people.)
- We stand against poverty and economic injustice and for dignified and decent economic conditions for all.
- We stand against tyranny and for democracy, justice, and the rule of law.[99]

Evangelicals for Social Action (ESA) is a project of the Sider Center on Ministry and Public Policy at Palmer Theological Seminary of Eastern University. ESA helps local churches develop and practice holistic ministry, combining evangelism and social action. ESA has also promoted international economic sanctions against apartheid, supported a multilateral rather than unilateral U.S. foreign policy, and endorsed many efforts to reduce poverty, promote racial justice, and care for creation.[100]

The Interfaith Alliance was created in 1994 to celebrate religious freedom and to challenge the bigotry and hatred arising from religious and political extremism infiltrating American politics. Today, Interfaith Alliance has 185,000 members across the country made up of seventy-five faith traditions as well as those of no faith tradition. The organization works at the national level to encourage interfaith dialogue, advocate for religious freedom, and fight against religious and political extremism, among other issues. Local affiliates mobilize individuals on the grassroots level to make a difference in their own communities. They offer a forum to challenge bigotry and defend religious freedom on local issues, including candidate education, religion in the public sphere, and interfaith relations.[101]

The Justice and Advocacy Commission of the National Council of Churches is a collaborative venture of America's community of ecumenical Christians who seek to be faithful in our day to the ancient prophet's call for all people of faith to seek justice. They address issues such as poverty, peacemaking, racial and gender equity and environmental stewardship.

The World Union for Progressive Judaism is the international umbrella organization of the Reform, Liberal, Progressive and Reconstructionist movements, serving 1,200 congregations with 1.8 million members in more than forty-five countries. Progressive Judaism is rooted in the Bible, especially the teachings of the Hebrew Prophets. Their website indicates that the union is founded on authentic manifestations of Jewish creativity, ancient and modern, particularly those that stress inwardness and desire to learn what God expects from us: justice and equality, democracy and peace, personal fulfillment and collective obligations. Tikkun olam (repairing the world) has been a core value of Reform Judaism throughout its history. The World Union seeks to mend, improve, and bear responsibility for the global community we live in through local as well as international social action and by instilling the value of tikkun olam in their youth.[102]

The Faith & Politics Institute is different from the above organizations in that they do not take specific stands on issues but rather facilitate dialogue between members of Congress and the faith community. The Faith & Politics Institute's website says that they "serve as the leading organization on Capitol Hill promoting effective government through reflective leadership, engaging members of Congress in opportunities for racial, religious and political reconciliation so that our leaders can take up the difficult and challenging issues of the nation in a constructive and bipartisan way" and that among those values it holds most important are: "Conscience, Courage, Compassion, Diversity, Integrity, Trust, Spiritual Engagement, Personal Reflection, Interfaith Understanding, Forgiveness, Civility, and Community." In an article on the website by staffer David TenBrook, he says, "our organization seeks to be a spiritual support system to those who do politics professionally. We hope to bring together the faith and politics of those who are often besieged by our nation's cynicism and lack of faith" and as a founder, Doug Tanner puts it, we hope to help elected leaders "hang on to a piece of their soul."[103]

Among the mainline denominations, the United Church of Christ (UCC) presents a notable example of faith-based social justice advocacy. The denomination's "Justice and Witness Ministries, one of four Covenanted Ministries in the UCC helps local congregations and all settings of the church respond to God's commandments to do justice, seek peace and effect change for a better world."[104]

The Christian Community Development Association (CCDA) is a network of Christians committed to seeking justice primarily through community ministry. As described on their website:

> We believe that God wants to restore us not only to right relationship with Himself but also with our own true selves, our families and our communities. Not just spiritually, but emotionally, physically, economically, and socially. Not by offering mercy alone, but by undergirding mercy with justice. To this end, we follow Jesus' example of reconciliation. We go where the brokenness is. We live among the people in some of America's neediest neighborhoods. We become one with our neighbors until there is no longer an "us" and "them" but only a "we." And, in the words of the Prophet Jeremiah, "we work and pray for the well-being of our city (or neighborhood)" trusting that if the entire community does well and prospers, then we will prosper also.

CCDA Practitioners make long-term commitments to living in an under-resourced neighborhood, often for ten years or more. They believe that true and lasting change takes time and requires real relationships. The CCDA philosophy is summed up by three "R's": Relocation, Reconciliation, and Redistribution.[105]

Even with the decline in the institutional church, the religious community is still the largest beneficiary of charitable giving and has tremendous property and other financial resources that can be pooled with private resources to create social justice ministries on a significant scale. It does involve risk taking, which much of the traditional church is reluctant to do. This provides a good transition to discussion of my congregation and the social justice work it has done on an interreligious public and private basis over the last forty years on behalf of "the least of these" in the Washington DC area.

Luther Place's Example of a Progressive Church's Collaborative Community Action to Foster Social Justice

As I mentioned earlier, my congregation, Luther Place Memorial Church in DC has been active in social justice for much of its history.[106] Formally known as Memorial Evangelical Lutheran Church, Luther Place was founded in 1873 as a memorial to peace and reconciliation following the Civil War. Two of the original pews were dedicated to Generals Grant and Lee. The statue of Martin Luther on our grounds (see below) was dedicated in 1884, on the four-hundredth anniversary of his birth. Much of the justice work through the years has been done on an interreligious basis, thus expanding the power of an individual congregation.

Luther Place Church (with statue of Martin Luther), Washington D.C.

As an interesting aside regarding my church's justice orientation, Luther Place went through a nave renovation project a few years ago, which included redoing our stained-glass windows. We already had a great representation of the church leaders since the Reformation on the existing stained-glass windows; these were preserved as is. However, the two front stained-glass windows had been replaced in a1960s renovation with very contemporary representations of Jesus and Martin Luther, and these were inconsistent with the historic character of the nave. The congregation decided to replace the windows to match the historic style but to add four progressive people of faith that represented Luther Place's contemporary message of social gospel and hospitality. After quite a bit of debate, we settled on Martin Luther, Martin Luther King Jr., Dietrich Bonheoffer, and Harriet Tubman. Thus the congregation, in two stained-glass panels, tells what its roots and vision are by highlighting these very important faith activists.

Following are examples of justice work during my time at Luther Place since 1968:

N Street Village

Nearly forty years ago, Luther Place created a model community for homeless and formerly homeless women at N Street Village just north of Thomas Circle across from the church on property it owned (see picture below). As one of the founders of N Street Village and a current board member, I want to share a bit more about the village and other social justice ministries at Luther Place:

N Street Village, Washington DC

Luther Place and an interreligious coalition gradually created the programs that became N Street Village. Luther Place opened its doors to the urban wounded during the days of fiery devastation after the assassination of Dr. Martin Luther King Jr. in April of 1968. In the early 1970s, the deinstitutionalization of chronic mental patients and bitter winter winds brought knocks on the door from wandering nomads seeking refuge. It was in this period that Luther Place began to consider its property and location as an opportunity to help minister to the wounded of the city. The Community for Creative Non-Violence (CCNV), the Sojourner Community, and Luther Place joined to open an emergency shelter for homeless in the Luther Place social hall. When CCNV and the Sojourners moved on after the first year, Luther Place congregation continued the shelters. Volunteers came from other churches of all traditions—especially the Roman Catholic Church

(Carmelites, Holy Trinity of Georgetown, and Blessed Sacrament of Bethesda), the Jewish community, and the Lutheran Church of the Redeemer in northern Virginia. The Luther Place chapel was later used to make separate safe space for women and, ultimately the upper floors were converted for permanent shelter space.

On the other side of N Street, Luther Place had already begun transforming row houses from the embarrassment of drugs and prostitution into what became a smorgasbord of "Matthew 25 ministries" (Bread for the City Center, Deborah's Place, Zacchaeus Medical Clinic, Sarah House, Bethany Women's Center, Dietrich Bonheoffer House, Abraham House, the DC Hotline, etc.). A multidenominational religious community led by Luther Place, with a Protestant, Jewish, and Catholic coalition (ProJeCt), created N Street Village and its ministries to women during these early years. This transformation was strongly influenced by the example and teachings of such peace communities as the Mennonites, Quakers, and Catholic Worker Movement, as well as by scholars such as Walter Brueggemann, Henri Nouwen, Abraham Heschel, and John Koenig (who all produced various writings on concepts of hospitality). For years, volunteers ran all of Luther Place/N Street ministries. The Mennonite and Jesuit Volunteer Corps provided inspiration for Luther Place's creation of the Lutheran Volunteer Corps. Those programs, along with AVODAH, the Jewish Service Corps, continue to send yearlong volunteers to work in N Street Programs. Increased funding support was gradually provided as contributions came from the larger community of congregations, individuals, foundations, corporations, and government.

Critical self-understanding of the early Luther Place and N Street ministries grew out of the rich traditions of Judaism and the New Testament tradition of welcoming the stranger, the outcast, the excluded of society. The way Luther Place and N Street opened doors to the homeless came to be seen by many as the essence of faith-based response to the critical needs of the community. This diverse interreligious and secular base of participants continues to this day, as people of many faiths and no faith live out the ministry of hospitality and shalom (peace with justice) in service at N Street Village.

Luther Place and its partners contributed significantly, financially and in many other ways, to the evolution of N Street programs. As N Street Village was forming and being built, Luther Place supported the financing. Luther Place also donated its Friends of Luther Place contributors' list, which at the time consisted of more than six thousand supporter names, generating nearly half a million dollars in annual income. Luther Place initiated, staffed (with a professional fundraiser), and managed the capital campaign to build N Street Village, raising about $19.5 million in capital gifts, including gifts through Friends of Luther Place. There was an initial $5 million federal capital grant to Luther Place for the building of N Street; we received over $5 million in low-income tax credit funding and were given significant corporate gifts and government loans, thus further broadening the base of support of N Street Village and its mission. Luther Place made its land available for the construction of the new N Street Village and in the process gave up its congregational parking lot. This was a complex public private partnership; Luther Place was assisted by some very wise counsel both within and outside the congregation for which we are eternally grateful.

N Street Village founders, John and Erna Steinbruck (pictured below near their home in Lewes, Delaware), and the Luther Place congregation created a vision and a challenge to the wider community that stirred contributions and funding to create N Street. Luther Place was insistent that the broad partnership and funding support that had been created be transferred to the "new" enterprise, with Luther Place continuing to provide essential underpinning. Today, N Street is larger than Luther Place can support by itself. As a separate 501(c)(3) nonprofit entity, N Street has attracted a more diversified board and funding sources than it could have as a subsidiary of a single congregation. Luther Place continues to view N Street as its progeny and provides a special place in its outreach program. Luther Place continues to provide a valuable bridge to the progressive religious community of the area, as well as to the history and religious roots of N Street. Luther Place's version of spirituality is as welcoming of the secularist as it is of the Bible-believing and those of other faiths. Luther Place will keep practicing and promoting that view of the role religious faith plays in public life. All who believe that it is our responsibility to "act justly and with love and compassion" (as taught by the prophet Micah) can find common ground in the faith inspired work of N Street Village.

John Steinbruck, our pastor at Luther Place for twenty-seven years, tells the story of how N Street Village evolved so much better than I could; here is John at his best:

It's simply not that complicated. It's Gospel 101. Yet, with "zillions" of square feet of unused churches' floor space, it's amazing to me how we, the church, can be so deaf to the cries of the homeless and blind to those whose hands reach up to us from city sidewalks. Our prolific theologians write their theologies, volume after volume, often requiring dictionaries to understand, yet obfuscate the obvious and simple Gospel.

"If your enemy is hungry, feed them." "Thou shalt not kill." "Peace, not war." It's just not complicated.

Yet some saw this as radical, even as the entire nation was being radicalized in the '70s. The revolution was right here at Thomas Circle, and the fragrance of tear gas was familiar. Practically every radical group you can think of had a 14th Street, Thomas Circle office in this corridor, from antiwar to nuclear freeze. I was connected with some of them, and some used space at Luther Place for meetings. There were times I'm sure when the congregation was unsure of what to make of such goings-on, but they were amazingly supportive—at once tolerating and even more, participating!

During that bitter cold winter of 1976, numbers of homeless were freezing and dying of hyperthermia. Together with Community for Creative Non-Violence (CCNV) and Sojourners, more than a thousand letters were sent asking other churches to join in opening their doors to the homeless. Not one response! Jesus said, "Come unto me all ye that labor and are heavy laden. Here in Luther Place you will be welcome to rest." What does that say about the church that has been mandated to welcome the stranger? This is a shared value of all the monotheisms: Christianity, Judaism, and Islam. In the Middle East, the stranger is considered "a messenger from God." I repeated these mandates a few times, and one Sunday after the service, the congregation voted to open the doors of Luther Place to all creatures great and small in whatever condition. On Monday night, we welcomed the strangers, opening God's doors and extending the biblical invitation "come unto me..." In twenty-four hours, we were wall to wall with the holy family of homeless thawing out in stairwells, in the social hall, even classrooms and the chapel. There is an efficient communications network on the streets. In came the poorest of the poor, the sickest of the sick, people infested with lice and scabies, paranoid schizophrenics, tubercular, and the unbathed crowded our floors, carrying the few things they owned in bags or carts. The church literally reeked of homelessness. Metropolitan Washington was stunned by this congregational action. But it was done! The faithful people of Luther Place opened the doors. We as a church had to make the biblical choice. The Bible says "Choose life, not death. Be a blessing, not a curse." Hallways, stairwells, the chapel, the social hall, and classrooms became "the Church as refuge!"

After 1976, there was no turning back. The homeless issue was squarely in our face. The concept of hospitality was a learning experience. Not just one Gospel text but "the Way" of Christ's life. The mission of Luther Place was hospitality, welcoming the stranger, Jesus. It was a gradual enlightenment that came along the road.

The other part of the message of the great Gospel prophets was to be advocates for social justice; to challenge the authorities, the "powers." I mean, here we were in the nation's capital, within blocks of the White House, and the contrast between there and here was dramatic. It meant, like Jesus and Moses, "community organizing." With the guidance of the Industrial Areas Foundation, we organized "one on one" throughout DC (read Rules for Radicals), and together, with a mass of organized congregations, challenged the powers of the city and the federal government. There were more than a few arrests. We even challenged our own Lutheran Church to come out from behind its suburban captivity, along with the church hierarchy, but the response was lame. They mostly looked the other way and saw us as something "radical"; which from a traditional church perspective we were. "Radical" is a good word that demands going to the roots of our problem as a nation in its great divide between extreme wealth and massive poverty. In our case at Luther Place, when stepping over homeless people to get to the church service, it's impossible to look the other way.

Luther Place dedicated the fourth-floor shelter in 1991 and Promise Place across the street in 1996. It was Erna who began to visualize the concept of a continuum of services for homeless women that would address their many needs on a journey from "homelessness to independence," accompanied by the various ministries on N Street. When Eden House/ Promise Place was dedicated, all those ministries came under a single roof. Our goal was to provide everything that was needed to bring women out of homelessness and into a full life. That included a day shelter, programs and classes, health and nutrition education and services, counseling, a floor to treat addictions, a floor for women dually diagnosed with both addiction and mental issues, and help finding a job and housing. Adjacent to Promise Place, part of the same large high-rise, is Eden House, which was designed to be part of that continuum. It has fifty-one low-income apartments to provide housing for women who have gone through Promise Place and found jobs that enable them to pay rent. HUD later adopted their own concept of "continuum of services" that was based on my wife Erna's idea demonstrated at N Street Village.

What we probably didn't realize is that we weren't anywhere near finished, but were just beginning a new and very challenging phase of N Street Village. We had already had to make so many huge decisions about the building—huge decisions about design, huge decisions about components of the building, like heating and air-conditioning. We had never done anything like that before—except for Henry Bowden, who was in real estate development and knew all that there was to know; like Abraham of old, we set out on a journey of raising $20 million (long story) toward a "promised place," a new place for those who had no place! Now we had other huge decisions to make about operating the building and programs. We had to hire a director for N Street Village. We soon realized that we couldn't be in the business of renting fifty-one apartments, so we had to hire a management company for Eden House. I remember we were meeting almost every night to figure it all out. And for the first year or two, we were losing money hand over fist. At this point, even though N Street was separately incorporated and had its own board, Luther Place was still carrying it. The congregation ended up loaning about

$1.8 million to N Street—completely depleting our reserves. It took two to three years until we were close to operating in the black and we transitioned to an interreligious N Street Board to cast a wide net for funding from DC foundations, corporations, and a "special" federal grant. And the story goes on, as N Street Village is nearing its fortieth year as a registered nonprofit in DC.

In fact, as I write, N Street is in an expansion mode. In October 2011, Miriam's House for women with HIV/AIDS became a part of N Street Village; the house on Florida Avenue Northwest has twenty-one units for women and children. In March 2012, N Street Village signed a contract with the city to operate a thirty-one-unit building at 1107 Eleventh Street, just four blocks away from N Street Village; this will be supportive long term housing for formerly homeless women. This is great news for our clientele!

Another key program started by Luther Place, the Lutheran Volunteer Corps, also emerged out of this challenging period of the late 1970s.[108] We were getting so much help from the Mennonite and Jesuit yearlong volunteers that Pastor John Steinbruck began to ask the national church if a Lutheran Volunteer Corps wasn't something it should consider. He presented the idea to the Lutheran Church of America in New York in 1976 and 1977. Conversations went back and forth, but nothing ever happened. So finally, in May 1979, on behalf of the Luther Place Council, I presented a resolution to the church to start a small Lutheran Volunteer Corps here, out of Luther Place. We called one of the Mennonite volunteers, Denise Snyder, who had done some intern work with us the year before, to take a half-time position with the church to help start the Lutheran Volunteer Corps. That first year we weren't fully organized to bring in yearlong volunteers, so we had a series of short-term volunteers who came during semester breaks and vacations. We looked at the Mennonite model and the Jesuit model and came up with our own program for Lutheran volunteers. In 1980, we had nine yearlong volunteers who stayed in what was called Bonheoffer House, located across the street from the church in a house that is now part of N Street Village. The Lutheran

Volunteer Corps still has its headquarters at Luther Place, and it now places nearly 150 volunteers in sixteen U.S. cities. They're all in social justice ministry of one kind or another. Some are with nonprofits doing advocacy on Capitol Hill; other programs deal with poverty, housing, homelessness, and a variety of issues. Nearly two thousand young people have now graduated from Lutheran Volunteer Corps, and many have gone on to become pastors or doctors or to work in nonprofit social justice programs around the country. It's just miraculous to see what this program has grown into from that small start with the nine volunteers we had the first full year. The 2011–2012 class of volunteers is pictured below.

Lutheran Volunteer Corps: Class 2011–2012

Photo by Ellie Grantson

Washington Interfaith Network (WIN) is yet another social justice community effort housed at Luther Place. Community-organizing models such as WIN are very effective in many cities in holding governments accountable for neighborhood action. The faith-based network's heritage includes democracy building and a focus on broad-based participation. The organization finds its roots in the work of Saul Alinsky, who founded the Industrial Areas Foundation during his organizing work in Chicago's working-class neighborhoods in the 1930s and 1940s. Known as the father of community organizing, Alinsky was committed to generating popular participation by those excluded from power. A core belief of these networks is that concrete community improvements follow from generating participation and training leaders to build powerful organizations committed to the needs of the families and communities that get involved. One of the hallmarks of faith-based community organizing is that, through it, people actively participate in civic and political action and don't just write checks to lobbying groups.[109]

WIN is a broad-based, multiracial, multifaith, strictly nonpartisan, district-wide citizens' power organization, rooted in local congregations and associations. WIN is committed to training and developing neighborhood leaders, to addressing community issues, and to holding elected and corporate officials accountable in Washington DC. A recent example is that they secured $200 million in new funding in the fiscal year 2009 DC budget to put neighborhoods first, including $117 million for affordable housing or permanent supporting housing, $55.8 million for recreation center upgrades, $169 million capital improvements for libraries, and $45 million in new funding for art and music teachers, literacy and math coaches, social workers, extracurricular activities, and athletics in DC schools.[110] In December 2011, WIN held a large rally in downtown DC (over two thousand people attended from congregations and nonprofit service providers) to advocate for greater attention to affordable housing and jobs. Efforts continue to challenge political leaders to follow through on commitments made at the December rally.

International Justice Issues

Luther Place has also collaborated in several international social justice issues, two of which I want to mention below:

1. Soviet Jewry: A great example of interreligious collaboration around an international justice issue was the daily Soviet Jewry protest vigil across from the Soviet Embassy in DC. The treatment of Soviet Jews had become an international issue by the late '60s and early '70s; the vigil in DC became a very

visible witness to their struggle. Bert Silver, one of the leaders of the vigil recently described the history:

> On December 10, 1970, Human Rights Day, a small number of Jews resolved to test the limits of the five-hundred-foot-rule limiting any protest within that distance of an embassy... The Jewish Community Council assigned a day each month to synagogues and organizations to have their members attend the vigil and people who worked downtown continued to attend frequently. Pastor John Steinbruck of Luther Place Memorial Church brought his parishioners to cover the vigil on Shabat and the Jewish holidays. At about that time, a lawsuit was filed attacking the constitutionality of the five-hundred-foot-rule, and eventually the court ruled that the rule was unconstitutional. The vigil then became a true community event. Notables and released refuseniks[ii] would attend and sometimes speak. Jews visiting from out-of-town knew it as a must event when visiting the city. Jewish organizations that held conventions in town would bring their delegates to stand there. The Soviet Jews knew of the vigil, and it was our understanding that the Soviet Embassy lodged a protest with our state department almost every day that the vigil was held. The vigil continued, uninterrupted, for over twenty years. The vigil was terminated in a ceremony on January 27, 1991, after it was clear that exit visas would be granted to any Jew wanting to leave the Soviet Union.[111]

In addition to participating with the Jewish community in the daily vigil, Luther Place adopted Soviet Jewish Prisoners of Conscience and advocated for their release from the Soviet Union. Pastor John Steinbruck of Luther Place also traveled with a Jewish delegation to Russia in the mideighties and was arrested with others of the delegation for bringing in illegal religious material and visiting with refuseniks in Moscow. This cooperation with the

---

ii Soviet Jews who were denied permission to emigrate

Jewish community resulted in additional interfaith collaboration, such as Jewish community support for N Street Village.

2. Another international justice issue is exemplified by the Rwanda ministry of Luther Place Church. In August of 2006, a small group from Luther Place traveled to Rwanda for two weeks at the invitation of Pastor John Rutsindintwarane, General Secretary of the Lutheran Church of Rwanda. Pastor John had spent six months at Luther Place in 2001–2002, studying approaches that would assist in rebuilding efforts among the Rwandan population following the 1994 genocide that took eight hundred thousand lives in a country with a population of eight million. We traveled there to learn about the reconciliation and community-building processes underway in Rwanda, helping both perpetrators and victims of the genocide to live peacefully together in this small East African country.

We experienced both the most tragic and most optimistic aspects of Rwandan life and talked to those at both the top and bottom of society. Regarding the tragic side, my most gruesome faith-testing experience was visiting a small church in Nyamata where five thousand people were killed during the genocide as they gathered in the church, assuming it was a place of sanctuary. It is now a genocide memorial. As a reminder of the horror and in the hope that it will never happen again, the bones and skulls of the victims remain on display in the church.

Overall, our deepest impression was one of profound hope and optimism, of new life growing from unbelievable horror. The society was at a critical juncture, and we committed to doing our small part to help sustain the work of recovery. Pastor John, since his return to Rwanda in early 2006, has focused on post genocide reconciliation and community development projects working with local congregations. In regard to reconciliation, the most profound experience was visiting a rural village where a former genocide perpetrator (see the man in dark shirt in center left of photo) was being integrated back into the village where he had helped commit atrocities. The two girls in the center of the picture are the daughters of parents killed in the village during the genocide, possibly by this perpetrator. Yet the village members, including the girls, were welcoming this perpetrator back into the village after he had served a prison sentence, repented to God and the village, and committed to helping build a better future for the community.

After our trip to Rwanda in 2006, Luther Place committed to help the rebuilding process in a number of ways, including providing support to Pastor John for fuel costs associated with his ministries of reconciliation around Rwanda, helping a rural Lutheran congregation in Kirehe construct a church building, assisting with development of a medical clinic in rural Mumeya village (more information below), funding student secondary-school scholarships, supporting the Rwanda School Project, and other related initiatives. Using community organizing techniques he learned during his internships at Luther Place and in Oakland, California, with People Improving Communities through Organizing (PICO), Pastor John particularly focused efforts on assisting congregations in rural Mumeya village in southeast Rwanda to come together to meet the community's most pressing need, which turned out to be health care. Mumeya village is twenty-five kilometers from any medical services, and no transportation is available. The community suffers from malaria, dysentery, tuberculosis, HIV/AIDS, early childhood mortality, and other debilitating health problems, but few can get to the distant health facilities. Our group visited the proposed Mumeya site in 2006 and heard firsthand about the community's health needs and how they had joined together to make this happen. We saw their plans and were impressed with the large pile of rocks that had been carried from considerable distances by the community to be used for the clinic foundation (see photo below of Luther Place members visiting Mumeya clinic site. Our host, Pastor John Rutsindintwarane is in the center right of the photo, shaking the hand of one of our delegation).

Luther Place congregation thereafter committed to providing transportation funds for Pastor John to travel weekly to the village for project oversight and to contribute building materials, which we have done annually through Advent Gifts of Hope. After more than two years of careful planning and preparation of the foundation, the community made good progress in construction of the clinic, the government assisted with construction and staffing, and the initial three rooms were in operation as an outpatient clinic in late 2009. When we visited again in August 2011, an additional four rooms were nearly completed (see picture below). The community strategy was to start small with their limited resources but gradually work toward construction of a larger medical facility that could have up to fifty beds. Most recently, Luther Place members designed and conducted fundraising for a solar electric system for the clinic, as there is no electricity in this remote village. Luther Place and other supporters raised fifteen thousand dollars, and combined with a contribution from the Rwandan village's mayor of used solar equipment that was no longer needed, the system is being implemented and will greatly enhance the service capabilities of the clinic. My wife, Margaret, and I traveled there in the summer of 2011, exactly five years after our previous visit, to assist with these projects. We were so impressed with the progress Rwanda has made in those five years. It has one of the fastest growing economies in Africa, and it is the most peaceful country in the region. Many nongovernmental organizations and diplomatic representatives are choosing to locate their families in Kigali, Rwanda, while they are on duty in other East African countries. It is truly inspiring to see such a success story and be a small part of it

4

Current Economic and Political Trends in the United States That Call Out for Progressive Action

The concept of the common good is central to the tenets of many religious faiths and can be succinctly described by the Golden Rule, that is, doing unto others as we would wish done unto ourselves. Aristotle is usually cited as the first to articulate an ethical understanding of the common good, followed by Augustine of Hippo and Thomas Aquinas, who developed the concept into standard moral theology.[112] Catholic social teaching in this regard is best summarized in Gaudium et Spes, issued by Pope Paul VI in 1965. [113] For example, number 30 says: "It is imperative that no one ... would indulge in a merely individualistic morality. The best way to fulfill one's obligations of justice and love is to contribute to the 'common good' according to one's means and the needs of others, and also to promote and help public and private organizations devoted to bettering the conditions of life." Three essential elements of the common good as defined in Catholic social teaching are:

1. Respect for the human person—made in God's image
2. Social well-being of the group and the development of the group
3. Peace, stability, and the security of a just order

Professor Michael Sandel of Harvard University says we need a new 'politics of the common good'. In a series of lectures delivered at Georgetown University in 2009, he challenges a market-based public policy focused primarily on using cost-benefit analysis; he advocates for a move back to politics that also considers moral and religious values; that is, considerations of the common good. For example, he says that health care should not be strictly a market consideration; most developed countries consider it a moral imperative to provide access to health care for everyone. He also believes that the inequality in incomes is the worst since World War II, and that this is destructive of the common good; it leads to extreme gaps between the privileged and the common person. He suggests that in this situation, public services also tend to decline because the well-off can buy their own schools, transportation, recreation, and so forth; a sense of community can be lost.[114]

I was pleased to see the Vatican's Pontifical Council for Justice and Peace issue a strong and thoughtful report in October 2011 on the current financial turmoil in both the United States and Europe; it spoke of ethics over the economy and embraced the logic of the global common good.[115] It supported increased international regulation to curb excesses of the financial markets and to place the common good at the center of international economic activity.[116]

In *The Great Awakening* Jim Wallis discusses seven "rules of engagement" for political involvement by Christians and other faith traditions; not surprisingly, one of these urges us to seek the common good.

1. God hates injustice.
2. The Kingdom of God is a new order.
3. The church is an alternative community.
3. The Kingdom of God transforms the world by addressing the specifics of injustice.
4. The church is the conscience of the state, holding it accountable for upholding justice and restraining its violence.

5. Take a global perspective.

6. Seek the common good.

I have selected the following issues that particularly stand out in our time as needing progressive social justice advocates to help achieve the common good:

Economic Justice

Marcus Borg, in his book *Speaking Christian*, says that "The U.S. is the most Christian country in the world yet we have the greatest income inequality of any of the developed nations. Our income inequality is literally off the charts. Moreover, income inequality has been growing for over 30 years. The wealthy have become more wealthy and powerful and the middle and lower economic classes have seen their well being decline—in the most Christian country on the globe." How do we reconcile this with the message of the gospel?

While income disparity in the United States reaches new highs, national and state budget cuts are often targeted to the most vulnerable while the wealthiest are protected. The richest four hundred Americans have more wealth than half of all American households combined; the effective tax rate on the nation's richest people has fallen by about half in the last twenty years. The Equality Trust provides social indicator comparisons among developed countries; their chart below shows that the United States has among the highest income disparity among developed countries, with the top 20 percent being more than eight times richer than the poorest 20 percent.

How much richer are the richest 20% than the poorest 20%?

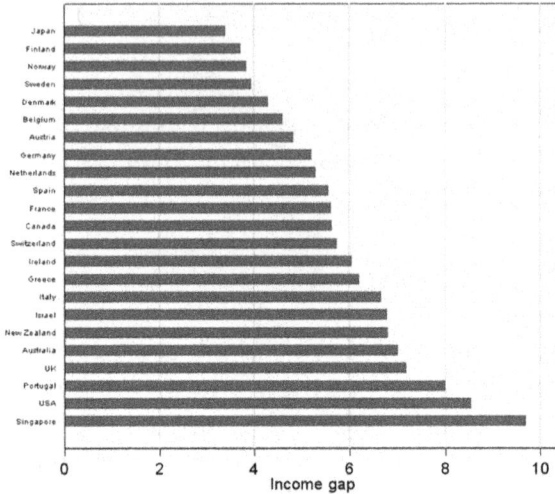

Income gap

Source: United Nations Development Program

Source: Wilkinson & Pickett, The Spirit Level (2009)

www.equalitytrust.org.uk   ~Equality Trust

This is not surprising given that the median executive income has increased 430 percent since 1980, while average worker wage income has increased 26 percent. Robert B. Reich, former Clinton administration Secretary of Labor, says in his recent book *Aftershock* that "None of us can survive in a nation divided between a small number of people receiving an ever larger share of the nation/s income and wealth, and everyone else receiving a declining share. The lopsidedness not only diminishes economic growth but also tears at the fabric of our society."[117] Social mobility, a long-cherished American dream, to be able to pick oneself up by the bootstraps, and advance economically in this country seems no longer possible for most Americans. A recent Organisation for Economic Co-operation and Development (OECD) study indicates that upward mobility was significantly lower in the United States than in most European countries.[118] So much for Conservative political claims about American exceptionalism. But we used to have much better social mobility in this country, so it is possible it will happen again. It will take good public education, health care and nutrition for all children, and improved infrastructure (including the information infrastructure) to connect all parts of the nation and more. But instead we are choosing to cut these vital programs, thus likely further stagnating social mobility in our country.

Further, the recent high unemployment only exacerbates the economic inequality issue. While the corporate sector rebounds, unlike previous recession recoveries, companies are not hiring new workers; this is puzzling. At the same time, it is interesting to note, according to a recent Department of Commerce report, that so far during the 2000s, multinational corporations based in the United States added 1.5 million workers to their payrolls in Asia and the Pacific region while cutting payrolls at home by 864,000.[119]

In the most recent year, corporate profits grew at their fastest rate since 1950, yet giant corporations like General Electric paid zero dollars last year in U.S. taxes on profits. Further, the Supreme Court recently ruled that corporations have First Amendment rights to free speech, thus allowing them to give unlimited amounts to candidates for office; presumably this new power will not be used for altruistic reasons. At the same time, these corporations are increasingly taking their headquarters offshore so they don't have to pay taxes here (60 Minutes, March 27, 2011). CBS further reported that: "An increasingly popular way, particularly pharmaceutical and hi-tech companies like Google, to avoid paying the 35 percent is to shift their patents, computer code, pill formulas, even logos from their U.S. bases to their outposts in low-tax countries."[120] U.S. Economist Martin Sullivan told Congress that these patent and profit transfers are accounting tricks that have allowed companies to lower taxes substantially below 35 percent; he said that from 2007 to 2009, creative accounting helped lower Pfizer's average tax rate to 17 percent, Merck to 12.5 percent, and GE to just 3.6 percent while profits were at new highs. At the same time, the median pay for top executives at two hundred big companies last year was over $10 million (the highest reported was nearly $85 million), a gain of nearly a quarter from 2009.[121]

Another egregious example is the carried interest loophole that benefits managers of financial partnerships, such as hedge funds, private equity funds, venture capital funds, and real estate funds— who are among the highest-paid people in the world. These fund managers are compensated mostly with performance bonuses. Under this carried interest loophole, the bonuses are eligible to be taxed at the long-term capital gains rate (if the fund's underlying assets are held long enough) of just 15 percent rather than the regular personal income rate of 35 percent. Closing the loophole won't fix the budget by itself, but it gets us one step closer to some sense of economic justice at a time when the richest 1 percent of Americans has a greater collective net worth than the entire bottom 90 percent of Americans. The larger question is whether we should try to balance budget deficits just by cutting discretionary programs for the most needy, or if we also need to seek some tax increases for those best able to afford them?[122] [123] Here is what Warren Buffett, a multibillionaire himself, has to say about the matter: "While the poor and middle class fight for us in Afghanistan, and while most Americans struggle to make ends meet, we mega-rich continue to get our extraordinary tax breaks. Some of us are investment managers who earn billions from our daily labors but are allowed to classify our income as 'carried interest', thereby getting a bargain 15 percent tax rate. Others own stock index futures for 10 minutes and have 60 percent of their gain taxed at 15 percent, as if they'd been long-term investors. These and other blessings are showered upon us by legislators in Washington who feel compelled to protect us, much as if we were spotted owls or some other endangered species. It's nice to have friends in high places."[124] Ironically, presidential candidate Mitt Romney was pressured by fellow Republicans to release his income tax returns recently. The reason for his reluctance to release them earlier was immediately obvious; he was the beneficiary of the carried interest loophole, which allowed his substantial income to be taxed at the 15 percent rate, thus leaving him with a lower tax rate than most ordinary Americans. To fix this type of loophole and bring more fairness to the tax code as Warren Buffett suggests, President Obama proposes in his 2013 budget to tax millionaires at a minimum 30 percent rate; this proposal is widely referred to as the "Buffet rule." It will be interesting to see if Romney(who pays tax rates at approximately 13 percent), like the Republican leadership in Congress, fights this proposal; it would seem to be a difficult position for a candidate who says he is looking out for the interests of the middle class.

The United States experienced two unprecedentedly long periods of sustained economic growth during the later 1980s and 1990s, yet most of the total increase in Americans' income went to the top 1 percent. The first decade of the twenty-first century saw productivity increase by about 20 percent. Yet virtually none of the increase translated into wage growth at middle and lower incomes. We know where it went: largely to CEO and top management salaries and to corporate profits.[125] The Institute for Policy Studies reports that the overall CEO-to-worker pay gap is exceptionally high by historic standards; Standard and Poor's 500 CEOs in 2008 earned 319 times more than the average worker.[126]

Francois Furstenberg, author of *In the Name of the Father: Washington's Legacy, Slavery, and Making of a Nation,* writes about the Gilded Age in the late nineteenth century, when wealth became similarly imbalanced: "Writer Henry George running for mayor on New York City in that period decrying the speculative gains of financial barons and the monopolists who appropriated unearned profits. The vast disparities between the rich and poor and the inability of the government to mitigate the crisis brought the nation to the edge of class warfare and social disintegration."[127] He further describes the labor protests that erupted all over the country. The excesses of the so-called robber barons helped foster the Progressive movement in the 1890s and led to President Teddy Roosevelt taking on the corporate barons of his day. Today, new fortunes have been accumulated that rival those of the Gilded Age. Some of the wealth of the current robber barons is being used to promote special tax breaks in Congress and lobby against financial regulation.

A key issue in regard to the recent financial meltdown is the lack of accountability for what happened. Wall Street is again fat and happy, yet not a single person has gone to jail for almost taking down our nation's financial system. The Financial Crisis Inquiry Commission set up to investigate the crisis reported its findings in January 2011. It concluded that the crisis was avoidable and was caused by: "Widespread failures in financial regulation, including the

Federal Reserve's failure to stem the tide of toxic mortgages; dramatic breakdowns in corporate governance including too many financial firms acting recklessly and taking on too much risk; an explosive mix of excessive borrowing and risk by households and Wall Street that put the financial system on a collision course with crisis; key policy makers ill prepared for the crisis, lacking a full understanding of the financial system they oversaw; and systemic breaches in accountability and ethics at all levels."[128] Greg Smith, a former Goldman executive, recently wrote a damming letter about the company's practices as he was walking out the door. He described a corporate culture that values only one thing: making as much money as possible, by whatever means necessary. He describes Goldman traders vying to see how much profit they could make at the expense of their clients, even if it meant selling them toxic products. "It makes me ill how callously people talk about ripping their clients off," Smith wrote.[129]

Congress was able to pass the Dodd-Frank financial regulation legislation in 2010, but now the legislation is under attack from the financial industry and their congressional supporters. Treasury Secretary Geithner says:

> There is still a great deal of work to do to repair damage caused by the crisis, and to implement the full framework of reforms...As we move forward, however, many of those who fought reform during the legislative process are now trying to slow down and weaken rules, starve regulatory agencies of resources, and bloc nominations so that they can ultimately kill reform. We will not let that happen. Too many Americans are still suffering from the pain of the financial crisis. We owe them a financial system with better protections against abuse and catastrophic risk.[130]

Ironically, the main provision of Dodd-Frank financial reform legislation that gave ordinary Americans some potential relief, the Consumer Financial Protection Agency, is relentlessly under attack by Wall Street barons and their Conservative supporters in Congress.

Columnist Harold Myerson describes how corporate America has a chokehold on worker's wages. He cites Michael Cembalest's (the chief investment officer of J.P.Morgan Chase) analysis, finding that U.S. labor compensation is at a fifty-year low relative to both company sales and U.S. gross domestic product, while profit margins of the Standard and Poor's 500 companies are at their highest levels in decades.[131] At the same time, as incomes have stagnated or dropped for middle- and lower-income Americans, the most vulnerable are again under attack, this time in the House budget bill, introduced by Paul Ryan (Republican, Wisconsin). According to the Sojourners website "The budget cuts proposed in the House…represent a 2.6% cut in total spending but at 26% cut in spending on poverty focused foreign aid. Many of the programs at stake once held bi-partisan support. The extension of Bush era-tax cuts last December will cost $6.7 billion through estate planning loopholes alone. Meanwhile, Congress is considering $7.6 billion cuts to domestic programs for low-income women, infants and children. And, the bill would increase defense spending."[132] At the same time, you can be sure that corporate lobbyists are protecting the interest of the fat cats.

Meanwhile, David Beckmann, president of Bread for the World, and his allies (more than thirty organizations are on board) are trying to protect the most vulnerable. Beckman says: "We shouldn't be reducing our meager efforts for poor people in order to reduce the deficit," they didn't get us into this, and starving them isn't going to get us out of it."[133] Beckman further said:"You can't have real religion, unless you work for justice for hungry and poor people." To address this challenge, Beckmann has helped form a new coalition, in which Bread for the World and Sojourners are key leaders, out of concern of the devastating effects that proposed budget cuts could have on vulnerable people. The Sojourners website noted above reports that: "This large coalition of Christian, Muslim, Jewish and other advocacy organizations have announced a broad based movement of fasting, prayer and advocacy, provoked by budget cuts proposed by Congress that would disproportionately hurt those living in poverty. Leaders of these organizations have joined in fasting, prayer and other acts of personal sacrifice…and inviting their constituencies—together representing millions of Americans—to do the same."

As we look forward, the situation is more perilous; as fewer Americans have defined pension programs, more and more will rely on Social Security. Unfortunately, Social Security will pay only about 39 percent of the average worker's preretirement earnings, which makes for a very meager retirement income given the stagnant wages in recent decades. Further, a recent Harris poll found that 34 percent of Americans have nothing saved for retirement.[134]

Globalization is often cited as a major cause of our job problems, but the picture is more complicated than that. We have benefited as a country by lower costs of goods with globalization, and developing countries have benefitted on their economies and their workers. So there have been mutual benefits with globalization, but recently we have seen the structural changes that have begun to impact the U.S. employment picture. The employment structure in the United States has been shifting away from the manufacturing sector, where developing countries are able to provide the basic manufacturing skills. The United States still controls the upper-end, high-value-added portion of the market. There are clearly benefits of free and open markets for producers and consumers but we will have to address some of the structural changes in employment in the United States through strategies such as education, training, and changes in corporate incentives. Germany has been the most successful of the developed countries in adapting to globalization. They have taken measures to foster and keep a significant part of their manufacturing base. As a result, the average income of the top 20 percent of the population to the average income of the bottom 20 percent is four to one in Germany as compared to eight to one in the United States.[135]

Meanwhile the news about poverty levels in America is bleak. Recent data published by the Census Bureau shows another 2.6 million people had slipped into poverty in the United States last year, and the number of Americans living below the official poverty line, 46.2 million people, was the highest number in the fifty-two years the bureau has been publishing figures on it. Counter to the usual stereotype, people in poverty do have jobs. The problem is that they don't have good jobs that pay enough to lift them out of poverty.[136] U.S. Senator Bernie Sanders (Independent, Vermont) says: "The crisis of poverty in America is one of the great moral and economic issues facing our country. It is very rarely talked about in the mainstream media. It gets even less attention in Congress. Why should people care? Many poor people don't vote. They certainly don't make large campaign contributions, and they don't have powerful lobbyists representing their interests."[137] And the Republican presidential candidates are shamefully pandering to the right wing of the party on this issue. Here is what former House speaker Newt Gingrich (and now presidential candidate) said about children in poverty at a recent campaign appearance in Iowa: "Start with the following two facts: Really poor children in really poor neighborhoods have no habits of working and have nobody around them who works. So they literally have no habit of showing up on Monday. They have no habit of staying all day. They have no habit of 'I do this and you give me cash' unless it's illegal." [138] [139] And Mitt Romney's recent comment on CNN that he doesn't worry about the very poor further highlighted the disconnect of the political debate from issues of poverty.

So in this worst recession since the Great Depression and with income inequality the worst in decades, what is the most recent offering by our presidential candidates? Mitt Romney promises to cut everyone's taxes, increase defense, and protect those currently receiving entitlement programs; so poverty-oriented programs are primarily what is left to cut. I guess he was sincere when he said "I don't worry about the poor." Former candidate Santorum proposed to flatten the tax structure and require drastic cuts in discretionary social programs to achieve the budget savings he claims he could make. Former candidate Herman Cain, in his 9-9-9 flat tax reform plan (9 percent income tax, 9 percent sales tax, and 9 percent business tax) proposed to reduce taxes on the most wealthy while increasing taxes for low- and middle-income citizens. An analysis by the Tax Policy Center showed that the bottom 20 percent of earners would pay over $1800 in additional taxes, while roughly half of those among the top 20 percent of earners would get an average tax cut of $14,400. Yet at the point in the campaign of releasing his 9-9-9 plan, Cain was the favorite with the Religious Right. It is extremely puzzling for the Religious Right to be supporting these candidates who are going so blatantly against biblical values (Jesus says that what you do unto the least of these. you do unto me) and against their own economic interests. It is counterintuitive for these moderate-income religious voters to be supporting a candidate and a plan that increases their taxes while cutting their benefits.[140]

Given the increasing poverty levels, some are advocating the concept of a living wage to improve economic justice. According to Wikipedia:

> Living wage is a term used to describe the minimum hourly wage necessary for an individual to meet basic needs, including shelter (housing) and other incidentals such as clothing and nutrition, for an extended period of time or a lifetime. In developed countries such as the United Kingdom or Switzerland, this standard generally means that a person working forty hours a week, with no additional income, should be able to afford a specified quality or quantity of housing, food, utilities, transport, health care, and recreation...The living wage is a concept central to the Catholic social teaching tradition beginning with the foundational document, *Rerum Novarum*, a papal encyclical by Pope Leo XIII, issued in 1891 to combat the excesses of both laissez-faire capitalism on the one hand and communism on the other. In this letter, Pope Leo affirms the right to private property while insisting on the role of the state to require a living wage.[141]

So why are the Catholic Bishops focusing most of their political energy on abortion, contraception, and gay marriage?

However, companies that pay their employees a livable wage along with benefits can suffer from opinions of Wall Street analysts and shareholders. For example, it's reported that the parsimonious approach to employee compensation practiced by Wal-Mart Stores, Inc. has made the world's largest retailer a frequent target of labor unions. In contrast, their rival Costco Wholesale Corporation often is held up as a retailer that does it right, paying well and offering generous benefits. But Costco's kindhearted philosophy toward its employees is drawing criticism from Wall Street. Some analysts and investors contend that Costco is actually too good to employees, with Costco shareholders suffering as a result.[142] So we as consumers, and in some cases shareholders, should counter Wall Street bias and vote with our pocketbooks by rewarding the companies such as Costco, which provide their employees a decent wage with reasonable benefits.

Economic justice will be critical both within our own country and around the world. In regard to world economic justice, Professor Paul Collier of Oxford University asks whether the "Bottom Billion" of the world's population will ever catch up. He characterizes this billion as living in about fifty countries, mostly in Africa, whose incomes have been virtually stagnant for the last fifty years. Meanwhile, the economies of the rest of the developing world have enjoyed accelerating growth. The income gap at the beginning of the millennium between the average citizens of the middle four-plus billion of the world's population and the bottom billion was five to one and increasing. He then describes the rest of us as the lucky billion—in Europe, North America, Japan and elsewhere—at the top. The bottom countries are mostly small; many are landlocked and therefore dependent on neighboring countries, and many are plagued by civil war. Globalization has left this billion behind. Collier says it's feasible to get the bottom billion on a more prosperous track, but doing so will require a serious approach that utilizes all the instruments at our disposal—and if sustained for many decades, it can have results similar to the Marshall Plan.[143] To President Bush's credit, he made a major commitment for AIDS victims in Africa through the Millennium Challenge Account. Unfortunately, current Republican presidential candidates are increasingly disparaging of foreign aid, so the near term outlook is not good for support to our brothers and sisters in places like Africa. Our church continues to support the Lutheran Church of Rwanda in reconciliation and community development after a disastrous genocide in 1994. We were most recently there in the summer of 2011 and saw remarkable progress with assistance from USAID, World Bank, European Union aid, and various nonprofit aid sources such as the Clinton Global Health Initiative. It would be sad to see regression on this kind of development aid.

Finally, we should come back to look for guidance in the scriptures, for if the Bible speaks loudly and clearly about anything, it talks about the need for a society to be equitable and just. As we are already seeing with the Tea Party on the right and the Occupy Movement on the left, when gross inequities are not dealt with effectively and fairly by government, enormous conflict is generated among a nation's citizens. Worst case scenario, this situation leads to violence. The potential for inequities to lead to social discord and violence is one of the reasons God's word speaks so clearly about the importance of fairness and justice in ruling a society. There are lots of ideas out there as to how we should fix our current inequities, including a few specific ones in the Bible. The Old Testament idea of the Jubilee Year argues strongly against the accumulation of wealth. Following Jubilee theology, every fifty years, wealth is to be broken up and distributed equitably. Jesus' suggestion that we give everything we own to the poor is just as dramatic.[144]

Human Rights

Human rights are generally thought of as basic rights and freedoms that all people are entitled to regardless of nationality, sex, age, national or ethnic origin, race, religion, language, or other status. Although the Declaration of Independence stated that we are all are created equal and have certain inalienable rights, it has been a long struggle for many groups within our society to fully realize these rights. Women's suffrage was a long struggle with support from the social gospel movement helping to accomplish women's voting rights in 1922. Later, the Equal Rights Amendment to the Constitution did not succeed, but women have made impressive gains in regard to equal protection in the workplace and other fronts. In regard to race, it has been a longer struggle. Despite the Emancipation Proclamation by Lincoln and the equal protection provisions of the Fourteenth Amendment in 1868, racial equality has been a long struggle. Nearly a hundred years after the Emancipation Proclamation, in 1949, theologian Howard Thurman wrote passionately in his book *Jesus and the Disinherited* about the continuing racial inequality in the United States. His book became an inspiration for Dr. Martin Luther King Jr. and the Civil Rights movement which resulted in the Civil Rights Act of 1964 and the Voting Rights Act of 1965 among other accomplishments. Despite impressive gains, issues of gender, race, human sexuality, and immigrant assimilation still tear at the fabric of American society. We only need to watch the various contenders for the presidency in 2012 trying to outdo each other in proposals to cut back such human rights!

The biggest battles in the United States are currently over human sexuality, immigration policy, and recently women's reproductive rights; these are often at the forefront of current political campaigns. The Don't Ask, Don't Tell ban on gays serving openly in the military was finally lifted in September 2011. During the eighteen-year practice, more than fourteen thousand service members were discharged from the military under this policy, thus losing valuable personnel at a time of critical national military need. The policy caused undue hardship for many fine service people; the one consolation for them is that their records can now be cleared, and they are eligible to reapply to the military. As with the positive effects of Harry Truman's integration of the military in 1948, this should be a very positive step for the nation toward ending discrimination based on sexual orientation. According to Gallop polling, a majority of Americans now support same-sex marriage rights, and among people ages eighteen to thirty-four (the so called millennials) support is at an overwhelming 70 percent. These demographic factors suggest that the legalization trend will continue. On the other hand, with the lifting of Don't Ask, Don't Tell in the military and the increasing liberalization of state laws regarding civil unions and gay marriage, conservatives, including Evangelical Christians, the Catholic hierarchy, and many Republicans are fighting back. Despite national Republican opposition, Governor Cuomo was able to bring some Republicans on board to help pass the recent New York legislation to allow same-sex marriage.[145] On the other hand, North Carolina with a Republican controlled legislature just passed a very restrictive constitutional amendment banning gay marriage and gay unions. Theodore Olson, the former Bush solicitor general, is reported to have told fellow Republicans "that a good same-sex marriage law embodies some of the party's most fundamental principles: freedom to live your life, stable families and religious liberty." President Obama recently grabbed the headlines with his announcement of support for same-sex marriage but he defers to the states on implementation. Same-sex marriage may soon be decided in the Supreme Court; it moved one step closer when a federal appeals court ruled in February 2012 that California's ban (Proposition 8) on gay marriage is unconstitutional, saying it serves no purpose other than to "lessen the status and human dignity" of gays.[146]

My wife and I are witness to the transformation that has taken place at our church Luther Place since we became a Reconciling in Christ congregation some fifteen years ago The Reconciling in Christ (RIC) Program recognizes Lutheran congregations that welcome lesbian, gay, bisexual, and transgender (LGBT) believers. Luther Place is blessed with many LGBT individuals and couples, including many with children; they have enriched our life at Luther Place immeasurably. We are so blessed by the diversity of our congregation, which, in addition to the large LGBT membership, includes racial and economic diversity by inclusion of women of N Street Village and others from the community.

In regard to immigration policy, attitudes seemed to have hardened in recent years. President Bush proposed comprehensive immigration reform, and he had the support of key republicans like John McCain but was unable to convince the broader Republican party. Now, even McCain has backed away from his previous stance in favor of reform. The current situation is untenable for the long term. Former governor of Florida, Jeb Bush, recently said: "I would argue that if we can't figure out how to control our border and move to a much more provocative and 21st-century immigration policy, the problems we face will become incredibly difficult to solve because we are not going to grow." Bush envisions an aggressive guest worker program. He also wants to see expansion of the H-1B visa program, allowing high-tech companies and others to recruit highly educated and motivated people from around the world.[147] The United States Conference of Catholic Bishops (USCCB) opposes "enforcement only" immigration policies and supports comprehensive immigration reform. In a letter entitled "Strangers No Longer: Together on the Journey of Hope," the U.S. Catholic Bishops outlined the elements of their proposal for comprehensive immigration reform.[148]

Another sensible proposal is the DREAM Act, sponsored by Senator Lugar from Indiana and Senator Durbin from Illinois, among others. The basic idea is to allow certain illegal immigrants who were brought here by their parents at a young age and who have been educated in American schools to become permanent residents. In essence, under the DREAM Act, certain undocumented individuals could become legal residents. The first step in this process is for the individual to enroll in some type of higher education, such as a university, vocational school, or apprenticeship program. Another option is to enroll in the U.S. military. If certain requirements are met, this person may apply for conditional residency in the U.S. Upon receipt of an associate degree or a two-year equivalent within six years of the initial petition, the conditional status can be changed, and the individual can become a legal permanent resident of the United States.[149] It was sad to see the Republican presidential candidates, including Mitt Romney, attacking Rick Perry at an early Republican presidential primary debate because he allowed in-state tuition for qualifying children of illegal immigrants to attend college in the state. Perry did the only sensible thing given that these children, through no fault of their own, are residents of the state of Texas and want to be productive citizens; Perry believes the state will benefit if these individuals become educated and contribute to society. Newt Gingrich was similarly attacked when he said in a CNN-sponsored Republican presidential candidate debate that: "I do not believe that the people of the United States are going to take people who have been here a quarter century, who have children and grandchildren, who are members of the community, who may have done something 25 years ago, separate them from their families, and expel them. I don't see how the party that says it's the party of the family is going to adopt an immigration policy which destroys families that have been here a quarter century."[150]

Worldwide, the oppression and abuse of women is still widespread. The United Nations Children's Fund (UNICEF) says violence against women, including genital mutilation, dowry killings, and domestic abuse is the most pervasive violation of human rights in the world today. The United Nations Population Fund says that "Millions of women across the world are beaten, killed, bought and sold by men, yet the gruesome violence and cruel treatment they face every day rarely makes headlines in the global media." They mention among the underreported stories "rampant domestic violence in Russia, sex slavery in India, self-immolation in Central Asia, gender-based violence and HIV, and "compensation" marriages in several parts of the world."[151] The brutal abuse of women and girls in the Congo (as part of the ongoing war there) is among the worst in the world; it is reported that in some villages, as many as 90 percent of the women have been raped; men in the villages are usually unarmed and therefore unable to fight back against armed perpetrators.[152] Within Islam, women continue to struggle for rights. For example, women in Saudi Arabia have been protesting by driving cars, a right that is denied to them by Saudi law. In response, a so-called scientific report has been released in Saudi Arabia suggesting that allowing women to drive cars leads to homosexuality and pornography. The report warns that giving women the freedom to drive would "provoke a surge in prostitution, pornography, homosexuality and divorce" and that within ten years of the ban being lifted, the report's authors claim, there would be "no more virgins" in the Islamic kingdom.[153] Women's rights are still an issue in many parts of the world. Fundamentalist elements of all three monotheistic religions tend to subjugate women, some in barbarous ways. U.S. religious figures attack such oppression of women in other societies, while women are still placed in a subservient role within many conservative denominations in the United States. This largely comes from a literal reading of the scriptures, which leaves cultural customs stuck in the same place they were two thousand or more years ago. Paul's writings (e.g., 1 Corinthians 11:2–10) implying subservience of women are particularly problematic. But progressive churches have come to a position of full inclusion of women through study and reflection on the scriptures as a whole and interpretation for our times. In regard to the equal role of women, progressive churches typically cite the following aspects of scripture, among others:

- Old Testament prophets call for justice, speak out against inequities, and stand with the oppressed.
- Jesus Christ had women as friends, disciples, and witnesses; he challenged the conventional beliefs of his day that women were inferior and men were superior.
- The Apostle Paul called the people of God to create a world where the gifts of both women and men are celebrated and used, where "there is neither male nor female, but all are one in Christ Jesus" (Galatians 3:28).

Decades ago, my denomination (the Evangelical Lutheran Church of America) embraced ordination of women and provision of full rights for women in all matters of the church. I am proud to say my congregation is led by two women pastors. Many other mainline denominations have also followed this path.

Within Catholicism, Vatican II offered hope for women, but as stated by Veronica Lawson, a Sister of Mercy and senior lecturer in theology at Aquinas Campus of Australian Catholic University, the post–Vatican II period has been a story of "one step forward and one step back" for women. Ultimately, she says, "The constraints imposed by papal teaching on the place of women in the church can only function as a powerful deterrent to any substantive change."[154] And now the Vatican recently issued a reprimand of American nuns and ordered a bishop to oversee a makeover of the organization that represents eighty percent of them; i.e. The Leadership Conference of Women Religious (LCWR).[155] The Vatican accused the nuns of pushing "radical feminist themes," and essentially said they were not vocal enough in mouthing church policy against the ordination of women as priests and against abortion, contraception and homosexual relationships. In effect, the Vatican accused the nuns of worrying too much about the poor and not enough about women's reproductive rights![156]

In another area of rights voting rights, state governments across the country have suddenly enacted an array of new laws and policies making it harder to vote. Some states require voters to show government-issued photo identification, often of a type that as many as one in ten voters do not have.

Other states made it much more difficult for citizens to register to vote, a prerequisite for voting. The array of new restrictions falls most heavily on young, minority, and low-income voters, as well as on voters with disabilities. This wave of changes may sharply tilt the political terrain for the 2012 election. Already nineteen new laws and two new executive actions are in place across the country.[157]

The other area of rights that has been under attack in recent years is the right to organize. Under international law, all workers have a human right to organize and to bargain collectively. These rights are an essential foundation to the realization of other rights, and are enshrined in the Universal Declaration of Human Rights. But in the United States, business interests represented by an increasingly conservative Republican Party have become much more assertive in fighting unions in recent decades. The most recent example was in Wisconsin, where newly elected Republican governor, Scott Walker, funded by corporate interests such as the Koch brothers and their Americans for Prosperity Foundation, successfully launched a broad effort to take away collective bargaining rights of public workers.[158] Corporate money continues to pour into Wisconsin to aid the governor who is threatened with a recall election. Walker complains that out-of-state individuals are coming to Wisconsin to help collect signatures for the recall initiative; however, he fully embraced corporate interests coming in from out of state to support his anti-union initiative. We see an interesting double standard being set by the governor.

Why is powerful out-of-state corporate money so intent on denying collective bargaining to public employees in Wisconsin? The answer seems to be to set an example that can be repeated in other states around the country. Fortunately, their aggressiveness backfired in Ohio, where a similar antiunion initiative was defeated.

Prison and penal reform is another area of human rights that is getting increasing attention. More than 2.3 million people, or one in every one hundred adults in the United States, are behind bars. Between 60 and 80 percent of individuals under supervision of the criminal justice system in the United States were incarcerated because of drug- or alcohol-related offenses and are disproportionately minorities. Many now see our so-called War on Drugs as a failure. The U.S. prison system costs taxpayers more than $60 billion per year, and facilities are bursting at the seams. Reforms are needed not only to reduce costs, but also to ensure fairness and humane treatment behind prison walls.[159] Nelson Mandela says "It is said that no one truly knows a nation until one has been inside its jails. A nation should not be judged by how it treats its highest citizens, but its lowest ones." The faith community is increasingly active in seeking prison and penal reforms.

Finally, there have been recent efforts toward severely restricting women's reproductive rights (e.g., contraception, prenatal exams, and abortion rights) despite the strong health reasons for birth control. The Centers for Disease Control and Prevention (CDC) lists the development of and improved access to contraception among the ten great public health achievements of the twentieth century, along with the development of smallpox and polio vaccines and public health campaigns to reduce tobacco use. Access to contraception has "contributed to the better health of infants, children, and women, and have improved the social and economic role of women."[160] Former presidential candidate Rick Santorum was quite vocal about contraception restrictions as he tried to appeal to the Religious Right. It seemed to backfire, however, as he lost both the Catholic vote and the women's vote in several primaries to Romney. Meanwhile, a proposed Mississippi statute last year would have defined personhood at conception, thus precluding certain types of birth control, in vitro fertilization, and first-term abortion. The measure was defeated because of these concerns, but the measure is sure to resurface in other states. Personhood USA, which pushed the Mississippi ballot measure, is trying to put similar initiatives on 2012 ballots in Florida, Montana, Ohio, and Oregon.[161]

Health Care

We advocate in many of our religious creeds the virtues of equality and justice, tolerance and compassion, but we perpetuate and live in a society where inequality has always been the norm. Health care is first and foremost a matter of love and compassion. Following the Faith Leaders Summit on Health Care in Washington DC in July 2009, the United Church of Christ issued a pastoral letter to all congregates, saying, "Health care is not only a basic human right but a human need. As people of faith we believe that it is a moral imperative to transform health care so that it is inclusive, accessible, affordable and accountable. We call on our churches to actively work towards the creation of a national health care system and to affirm the moral and justice imperatives of equal access for all people." U.S. efforts to achieve universal health coverage began with Theodore Roosevelt, who had the support of progressive health care reformers, including the Social Gospel movement, in the 1912 election, but the Progressives were defeated. So it was in the Progressive tradition that President Obama campaigned for and successfully passed health care reform. The president signed the Patient Protection and Affordable Care Act into law in March 2010.

But it has been under attack from the beginning from the Conservatives as an overreach of government authority. Virtually all Republican candidates now run on a platform of repealing health care reform without offering any viable options for insuring the nearly 50 million uninsured, dealing with access for those with preexisting conditions, and so forth. Mitt Romney, the current front-runner in the Republican primary race, is in a very difficult position on this issue, as the federal health legislation (including the individual mandate) is largely modeled after the Massachusetts health legislation enacted by Governor Romney. He enacted a progressive new law providing universal health coverage in 2006, which helped the uninsured buy private insurance, created a market-oriented insurance exchange, and required everyone to carry health insurance. As late as 2009, Romney championed the goal of providing health insurance to all Americans and cited his achievement in Massachusetts as coming close to achieving that goal. As these were long-advocated Republican positions (including the Republican health plan presented as an alternative to the Clinton health plan in 1994), most Conservatives, including the Heritage Foundation (considered the originator of the mandate idea), praised the Massachusetts plan at that time. However, when it largely became the model for national health reform launched by the Obama administration and a Democratic congress, Republicans largely switched sides and opposed it as a government takeover of health insurance.[162] Without strong support from hospitals and physicians, including the American Medical Association, which had opposed all previous efforts, Obama's health care legislation would have failed. Importantly, the Catholic Health Association, representing Catholic hospitals and led by Sister Carol Keehan, also supported the legislation even though the U.S. Catholic bishops did not. Sister Keehan is quoted as saying that "the legislation would provide health care to more than 30 million poor people and ease costs for everyone else."[163] Yet opponents shamelessly attack the legislation without offering any viable alternative for the millions of uninsured, including those with preexisting conditions. The one person who has successfully implemented such legislation at the state level, presidential candidate Romney, is forced to run away from his success in Massachusetts because his party's only platform for the future is to kill anything that might be a success for Obama. This is truly a sad state of affairs for the future of our country.

A key reason for national health care reform continuing to be on the national agenda is that in multiple analyses of developed countries, health care outcomes show the United States lagging far behind other developed countries. The United States spends 17 percent of its gross domestic product on health care, while other advance nations spend 10 to 11 percent; most of those other nations insure everyone, while we have nearly 50 million uninsured. For The United States doesn't have better health outcomes to show for all the spending we do on health care.[164] Comparative analyses (see World Health Organization, OECD, and Commonwealth Fund analyses) using different health outcome measures generally show the United States ranking somewhere between fifteenth to thirty-seventh in the world ranking of significant health outcomes, like infant mortality, healthy life expectancy, and health access and quality measures, as summarized in *The Healing of America: A Global Quest for Better, Cheaper, and Fairer Health Care* by T.R. Reid.[165] A forthcoming book on health care by Paul Starr, *Remedy and Reaction*, notes that in 1970, the United States spent a smaller fraction of income on health care than Denmark and the same share as Canada.[166] Today, in dollar terms, we spend two and a half times the average per capita of other rich countries. So don't let any politician tell you that our system is just fine or that, as some politicians insist, it is the best in the world; —he or she is lying to you.

There are huge inefficiencies in our health-care system, including problems with recordkeeping, lack of connectedness of information, and paperwork involved with so many different payers. We may eventually have to go to a single-payer system to avoid this inefficiency. The single biggest cost that most other countries don't have is insurance company profits of 20 percent or more off the top. Most countries have insurance entities that operate as nonprofits, thus immediately saving this huge slice of the cost. The other countries also benefit from using unified models of health care, although those models vary quite a bit. Unified systems make it easier to use digital recordkeeping and smart cards, thus cutting administrative costs. Our system, unfortunately, is a hodgepodge of government and private systems that don't share information. President Obama's economic recovery legislation included major funding and requirements for electronic health records, and this is expected to greatly enhance information sharing and improve care coordination over the next several years. Also, according to an article by Peter Orszag, former OMB Director, there are a number of options for cutting costs, and some are built into health care reform legislation signed by President Obama, including the Patient-Centered Outcomes Research Institute, a nonprofit organization that will help prioritize and fund new research on cost effectiveness of various treatments. Sharing of this information with providers helps make improved clinical decisions. Another improvement in the legislation are Accountable Care Organization models, which tie doctors and hospitals together in networks and provide incentives to deliver better care on a coordinated basis. Finally, the Independent Payment Advisory Board starts up in 2014, which is a panel of health care experts that will be responsible for making proposals to reduce growth in Medicare costs. Recommendations get implemented automatically unless Congress specifically overrides them in legislation that the president must also sign. [167]

I would be remiss if I did not comment on the current controversy over coverage of contraceptives in the new health care reform regulations being issued by the federal government. I sincerely respect the Catholic Church for all the great social justice work in this country, and throughout the world, in providing social services, health care, and aid to the poor. However, I strongly disagree with the Catholic Bishops and others opposing the new health care rules which provide that insurance plans include reproductive health care, including contraception. The Bishops have full right to preach against contraception in their parishes, but I don't think they have a right to prohibit important insurance coverage for more than a million employees of Catholic hospitals and other public institutions, such as colleges, which are engaged in regular commercial interstate public services. The same is true whether the hospitals are Catholic, Adventist, Baptist, or Methodist; they are all competing in the public marketplace to offer health services and therefore must abide by reasonable rules of the insurance marketplace. Somehow, the basic facts have gotten lost in most of the discussion. The regulation at issue simply requires that preventive health care services, which must be covered by employer health insurance policies under the Affordable Care Act, include contraception. It does not require anyone to use birth control. It specifically exempts churches and any religious employer that primarily hires and serves its own people. Although it applies to religiously affiliated hospitals and universities that serve the public and engage in interstate commerce, no Catholic hospital must itself provide contraception or family planning services to their employees or patients.[168] Most overlooked is the fact that Catholic and other religious-based hospitals have complied with similar rules concerning contraception coverage already in place in twenty-eight states and, as mentioned above, the Catholic Health Association (representing Catholic hospitals) supports the new health care legislation and agrees with the compromise the president proposed on this rule. So the rule only formalizes what is already practice, and the Catholic hospital's association supports the rule as revised. What is the issue?

The features of health care reform should significantly improve cost control, but they remain controversial and could still face challenges, as do other parts of the legislation. The individual mandate is probably the feature most under attack from Conservatives because it is the key to universal coverage. Being the most important feature of the reform legislation, it has been challenged in lower courts and gone to the Supreme Court for hearings in March 2012. Many associations, including the American Hospital Association and the Catholic Health Association (representing Catholic hospitals) filed briefs to the Supreme Court in support of the mandate. A decision by the court is expected in late June 2012.

Universal coverage is a basic goal we should continue as a first priority; most all advanced countries set this as a primary goal for their societies, and it is important to helping manage costs. Health care reform will continue to be a key issue for Progressives as legislative and court challenges continue to emerge. Should major provisions of the Affordable Care Act be struck down by the Supreme Court, we are left with the same patchwork mess that was not working before the legislation was approved. Given that the opposition doesn't offer a credible alternative, repeal is likely to lead us eventually toward some type of single-payer system in order to control costs and provide relatively universal coverage. It is interesting and ironic to note that Conservatives had come up with the idea of the individual mandate a few decades ago as an alternative to liberal Democrats who wanted a single-payer system.

Conflicts between Science and Religion

Hundreds of years ago, people thought the earth was unique and situated at the center of the universe. Today, according to one of our foremost scientists, Stephen Hawking (author of *The Grand Design*), we now know there are hundreds of billions of stars in our galaxy and hundreds of millions of other galaxies in the universe, thus leaving the earth as a small planet in a relatively ordinary galaxy of our massive universe. Further, Hawking postulates that there are many universes, each with their own sets of physical laws, histories, and many possible states. Finally, astronomers are increasingly discovering planets that seemingly have favorable conditions for life, like Earth, further diminishing the historic view that we had a unique position in the universe. These types of scientific findings regarding our origins and our position in the universe have historically been threatening to the church and the faithful. To me, as member of a progressive Christian church, these scientific discoveries only suggest a bigger God than we ever before imagined; one not bound by our limited view of space and time. One of the foremost scientists of the ages, Einstein, said; "That deeply emotional conviction of the presence of a superior reasoning power, which is revealed in the incomprehensible universe, forms my idea of God."[169] But as we recognize that there is continuing tension between science and religion, let's explore these issues a bit more.

As summarized in Wikipedia:

"A variety of historical, philosophical, and scientific arguments have been put forth supporting the idea that science and religion are in conflict. Historical examples of religious individuals or institutions promoting claims that contradict both contemporary and modern scientific consensus include creationism, the Roman Catholic Church's opposition to heliocentrism (theory that the sun is at the center of our solar system)...including the Galileo affair, and more recently, Pope Benedict XVI's 2009 statements claiming that the use of condoms to combat the AIDS epidemic in Africa was ineffective and counterproductive. On the other hand, scientific and theological perspectives often coexist peacefully. Non-Christian faiths have historically integrated well with scientific ideas, as in the ancient Egyptian technological mastery applied to monotheistic ends, the flourishing of logic and mathematics under Hinduism and Buddhism, and the scientific advances made by Muslim scholars during the Ottoman Empire. Christian Theology—excluding those fundamentalist churches whose aim is to reassert doctrinal truths—has likewise softened many of its ontological claims, due to increased exposure to both scientific insights and the contrasting theological claims of other faiths."[170]

For example, the Catholic Church now accepts the fossil history of evolution although it may differ over the pace and mechanisms of evolution.

The *Tammy Kitzmiller, et al. v. Dover Area School District, et al.* case heard in 2005 in Pennsylvania was the first direct challenge brought in the United States federal courts against a public school district that required the presentation of intelligent design as an alternative to evolution. The plaintiffs successfully argued that intelligent design is a form of religiously based creationism and not science, and that the school board policy thus violated the Establishment Clause of the First Amendment to the U.S. Constitution.[171] Although the judge's decision against creationism and intelligent design would seem to have put a nail in the coffin of efforts to rewrite high school science curriculums to include creationism approaches, the trial sparked considerable response from both supporters and critics, and the issue is far from settled. Recent polling shows that nearly half of Americans still believe in creationism, so the issue is not about to go away.

Further, the Unites States' lead in scientific education and research is threatened. Continuing attacks on public schools over the issue of teaching evolution results in watering-down of our science curriculums. Another example where Religious Right attacks on science are diminishing our scientific competitiveness is in the area of stem cell research. The National Institutes of Health only recently opened up new stem cell research lines after an eight-year restraint under the Bush administration. To include a personal example of the impact of such restraints on scientific research, a close friend of mine has been diagnosed with onset of Alzheimer's disease. After extensive medical inquiry, my friend decided to go to Korea for stem cell treatments; they appear to be well ahead of us in stem cell research and treatments for various diseases such as cancer, Parkinson's, and Alzheimer's. This is a sad commentary on U.S. scientific research, which was once the best in the world in most fields.

Can science and religion be compatible? Our latest scientific understanding is that it took around 14 billion years for all of the natural processes of creation to occur, which are presented so briefly in Genesis. The entire universe, including the earth and mankind, evolved in a natural evolution of events, according to our best understandings of science. With this scientific picture of our universe and its evolution, what is the place for religion? According to the National Academy of Sciences:

Acceptance of the evidence for evolution can be compatible with religious faith. Today, many religious denominations accept that biological evolution has produced the diversity of living things over billions of years of Earth's history. Many have issued statements observing that evolution and the tenets of their faiths are compatible. Scientists and theologians have written eloquently about their awe and wonder at the history of the universe and of life on this planet, explaining that they see no conflict between their faith in God and the evidence for evolution. Religious denominations that do not accept the occurrence of evolution tend to be those that believe in strictly literal interpretations of religious texts. Science and religion are based on different aspects of human experience. In science, explanations must be based on evidence drawn from examining the natural world. Scientifically based observations or experiments that conflict with an explanation eventually must lead to modification or even abandonment of that explanation. Religious faith, in contrast, does not depend only on empirical evidence, is not necessarily modified in the face of conflicting evidence, and typically involves supernatural forces or entities. Because they are not a part of nature, supernatural entities cannot be investigated by science. In this sense, science and religion are separate and address aspects of human understanding in different ways. Attempts to pit science and religion against each other create controversy where none needs to exist.[172]

In fact, many well-known historical figures who influenced Western science, such as Copernicus and Galileo, considered themselves Christian. Dr. Elaine Howard Ecklund, assistant professor of sociology and associate director for the Center on Race, Religion and Urban Life at Rice University believes that both science and religion are important in people's lives and that communication between religion and science is very important. She conducted research over a three-year period, from 2005 to 2008, where she learned, after studying three hundred academic scientists, that most of them have some degree of religious interest and belief. At least 50 percent maintain consistent belief and adherence to their faith. In fact, she reported that 68 percent have some sort of compatibility in their beliefs on science and religion. So instead of a lack of compatibility between science and religion, Ecklund found good reason to believe that there is a level of agreement where the scientific community can reach out and begin to dialogue with people of faith. The Monkey Bible project (book by Mark Laxer and music produced by my son, Eric Maring, http://www.monkeybible.com/) also explores the debate between science and religion. The novel is respectful of both sides and strives to provide a gentle, supportive bridge across which people who disagree can communicate.

Albert Einstein, one of the greatest scientists ever known, wrote an article about this very subject because he was concerned about both religion and science and the need for dialogue. This great scientist had an inquiring mind not just for science but for matters of faith as well. He looked at the fact that the major religions all have some idea of a God. Indeed, Einstein believed that an important motivating factor for the study of science of some of the greats had to do, in fact, with faith. Einstein wrote: "Only one who has devoted his life to similar ends can have a vivid realization of what has inspired these men and given them the strength to remain true to their purpose in spite of countless failures. It is cosmic religious feeling that gives a man such strength. A contemporary has said, not unjustly, that in this materialistic age of ours the serious scientific workers are the only profoundly religious people."[173]

Given Ecklund's research and Einstein's comments, it would seem reasonable that more dialogue between science and religion should take place. As Ecklund declares, if they don't, there is real danger for democracy and for the future of the entire world. Progressive churches have a key role to play in helping foster this dialogue. Because they are not constrained to literal translations of the Bible, progressive churches are often freer to open dialogue between seemingly opposing camps. So what can we do? The Lutheran (ELCA) Campus Ministry website has suggested resources and ways to start a dialogue on science and religion. The website's address is listed in the endnotes.[174] Another way is to participate in Evolution Weekend each February, when congregations from many different denominations participate in various ways. Evolution Weekend is an opportunity for serious discussion and reflection on the relationship between religion and science, but this effort goes on throughout the year. The site describes the effort as "An ongoing goal is to elevate the quality of the discussion on this critical topic, and to show that religion and science do not have to be adversaries. Instead, the information and understanding gained through legitimate scientific inquiry can be of significant help to people of faith in better understanding this wonderful planet that we live on - its beauties and wonders, as well as the many environmental threats to the health of both natural and human communities. Science can thus be of assistance to religious leaders and communities, as they seek to fulfill their calling to care for the Earth, through more informed advocacy and actions."[175] Progressive churches should also be engaged in school board or legislative battles at state and local levels where fundamentalists try to influence public school science curricula, for example, to teach concepts such as intelligent design as an alternative to evolution. It can also be extremely helpful for religious voices to be in dialogue with scientists as societal issues such as stem cell and human genome research and other controversial scientific and medical research issues are debated in public forums.

I place a lot of blame for anti-science attitudes on politicians who are pandering to the electorate rather than helping to educate. I am totally puzzled by the current crop of presidential candidates who are largely science deniers and yet want the United States to be an exceptional country. We are falling behind as world leaders in many fields of scientific and technological advancement because we are not investing in science education and research, and far too many of our children are being exposed to antiscience beliefs and concepts (e.g., creationism, which suggests that the earth and all its inhabitants were created by God within the last ten thousand years). I know of no nation that comes close to being a world leader without producing leading scientists in many fields of inquiry and is among the leaders in new patents and Nobel Prize winners. Yet our politicians and their Religious Right supporters routinely deny scientific findings of our best scientists and the collective findings of our national science academies. For example, over the past eighteen years, the U.S. National Academy of Sciences has produced more than forty scientific reports and studies on climate change. The most recent report concludes, "Climate change is occurring, is very likely caused by human activities, and poses significant risks for a broad range of human and natural systems." The world's major national scientific institutes, including the official academies of Australia, Belgium, Brazil, Canada, China, France, Germany, India, Japan, Mexico, Russia, and the United Kingdom, have independently published concurring conclusions. Yet in the current political season, only John Huntsman and President Obama among the recent slate of presidential candidates have refused to bow to the science deniers. The other candidates routinely deny science and attack the so-called elites who promulgate such ideas, by which they usually mean those who have advanced degrees from Ivy League or equivalent universities who try to force their ideas on the rest of Americans out there in the hinterlands.

In his latest book, *Unscientific America*, Chris Mooney says:

> Climate change, the energy crisis, global pandemics, nuclear proliferation—many of the most urgent problems of the twenty-first century require science-based solutions. Yet

Americans are paying less and less attention to scientists. For every five hours of cable news, less than a minute is devoted to science; the number of newspapers with weekly science sections has shrunken by two-thirds over the past several decades. Just 18 percent of Americans personally know a scientist to begin with, and exceedingly few can name a living scientist role model. No wonder rejection of science is rampant: 46 percent of Americans deny evolution and think the Earth is less than 10,000 years old; large numbers ... continue to attack the science of climate change; and the public—including its wealthiest and best educated sectors—is in dangerous retreat from childhood vaccinations.[176]

The evolution of species is indisputable from fossil evidence and human genome work developed by our leading scientists, yet many of our recent candidates for the highest office in our nation continue to deny evolution. The fact that Earth is not the center of the universe was settled by Copernicus in the sixteenth century, yet many hold to such antiquated beliefs. Our nation's lead in space and astronomy was made possible by previous investment in scientific education, research, and space exploration through manned, unmanned, and telescopic advancements that have allowed us to make tremendous strides in recent decades. Our advanced telescopes (e.g., the Hubble Space Telescope) now allow us to probe so deep into space that we are seeing objects less than 1 billion years from the big bang of 13.7 billion years ago. We know the earth and its Milky Way galaxy are far from the center of the universe; earth evolved about 4.5 billion years ago, with intelligent life evolving in the last 100 million years. Yet a poll taken recently by LifeWay Research (a Christian evangelical resource organization) of our nation's Protestant pastors found that over half did not believe in evolution. Ed Stetzer, vice president of research and ministry development for LifeWay Christian Resources was quoted as saying "Protestant pastors are overwhelmingly creationists and believe in a literal Adam and Eve."[177] These are leaders who influence many of our nation's youth and almost certainly would discourage many of them from pursuing advanced scientific or engineering fields at our leading universities because such education could threaten their rigid religious views.

At the same time, our country is falling behind in science, research and development, and high-tech jobs. The *Wall Street Journal* reports that large global companies are setting up research labs worldwide, where engineering and scientific talent is emerging.[178] According to a report of the National Science Foundation, about 56 percent of the world's engineering degrees awarded in 2008 were in Asia, compared with 4 percent in the United States; moreover, a large number of the engineering students are foreigners; 57 percent of U.S. doctoral degrees in engineering in 2009 went to foreigners, mostly students from East Asia or India.[179] If we continue to fail to motivate U.S. students to pursue advanced engineering and scientific degrees, we most certainly can't maintain a competitive edge in global research and technology, and thus more high-skill jobs will go to other parts of the world. Our presidential candidates all talk about how they will create jobs in this country, yet many espouse antiscience attitudes that will likely result in the continuing erosion of high-skilled jobs in the United States. Former presidential candidate Rick Santorum attacked President Obama for being a "snob" because of his aggressive goal to get more U.S. students into college, including community colleges where they can learn technical skills. Santorum claims that our universities are indoctrination mills that harm the country. What kind of babble is this? Santorum and his wife both have advanced degrees from nationally respected universities. Why would he want to deny this path to our young students?

Environmental Issues

Global warming is becoming an increasing threat to the survival of the planet. Population explosion in some of the developing countries, such as India, poses a sustainability challenge. China's rapid development and automobilization poses a huge challenge as well. Margaret and I spent nearly a month in China in September 2009. The infrastructure investment is incredible, and it is helping sustain double-digit economic expansion but also resulting in rapid increases in atmospheric pollutants. Further, rapid consumption of natural resources in both the developed and developing world is not sustainable.

Our leading scientists advise that we need to take global warming seriously, pointing out that the growth in global carbon dioxide emissions, if not curbed, could have disastrous implications for the planet and our species... Before the Kyoto protocol, 550 ppm was considered a rough upper limit before we would face devastating consequences of warming. The preferred target is now closer to 450 ppm, but it would take a global commitment of the developed and developing countries to enforce that, and neither seem to have the appetite for major constraints on growth and behavior. For the last ten thousand years, carbon dioxide levels were relatively stable at 280 ppm (parts per million). That suddenly changed with the Industrial Revolution, particularly in the last fifty years. Carbon dioxide emissions have shot up to about 385 ppm and are projected to climb by 2 to 3 ppm annually.[180] I personally worked on President Clinton's climate change initiative in 1994, when it was demonstrated that we could hold to 1990 levels of CO2 emissions using known technology. Improving vehicle efficiency was at the centerpiece of the effort; unfortunately, such efforts were blocked by Congress, and we lost another thirteen years until late 2007, when Congress and the president finally passed an energy bill with increases in vehicle fuel efficiency standards up to 35 miles per gallon by 2020. President Obama has upped that goal in subsequent negotiations with the automobile industry and environmental interests. Unfortunately, efforts to enact climate legislation have faltered, as an increasing number of citizens and politicians have become deniers, despite the fact that our nation's and world's best scientists are largely in agreement regarding climate change and its challenge to our planet.

The National Academy of Sciences recently released an important report on this topic, entitled "America's Climate Choices."[181] The report finds that the significant risks that climate change poses to human society and the environment provide a strong motivation to move ahead with substantial response efforts. Current efforts of local, state, and private-sector actors are important, but they are not likely to yield progress comparable to what could be achieved with the addition of strong federal policies that establish coherent national goals and incentives and that promote strong U.S. engagement in international-level response efforts. The inherent complexities and uncertainties of climate change are best met by applying an iterative risk-management framework and making efforts to: significantly reduce greenhouse gas emissions; prepare for adapting to impacts; invest in scientific research, technology development, and information systems; and facilitate engagement between scientific and technical experts and the many types of stakeholders making America's climate choices. This report came from a panel of our best U.S. scientists, yet the nation has gone into climate denial. It is pathetic to see national political candidates backtrack on previous climate change positions in order to gain support from the Political and Religious Right. The U.S. Congress is playing this dangerous game as well, by fighting even modest rules by the Environmental Protection Agency that would not only stem energy use and greenhouse gas emissions but also offer health benefits from reduction of toxic gases. This seems like a win-win-win but apparently it doesn't look that way to deniers. Where is the voice of the common good?

Meanwhile, new evidence is pointing to very real consequences of warming within our lifetimes and certainly within our children's and grandchildren's lifetimes. According to a new climate study by Stanford University scientists, the tropics and much of the Northern Hemisphere are likely to experience an irreversible rise in summer temperatures within the next twenty to sixty years if atmospheric greenhouse gas concentrations continue to increase. In the study, the Stanford team concluded that many tropical regions in Africa, Asia, and South America could see "the permanent emergence of unprecedented summer heat" in the next two decades. Middle latitudes of Europe, China, and North America—including the United States—are likely to undergo extreme summer-temperature shifts within sixty years, the researchers found. "This dramatic shift in seasonal temperatures could have severe consequences for human health, agricultural production and ecosystem productivity," said study leader Noah Diffenbaugh. As an example, he pointed to record heat waves in Europe in 2003 that killed forty thousand people. He also cited studies showing that projected increases in summer temperatures in the Midwestern United States could reduce the harvest of staples, such as corn and soybeans, by more than 30 percent. Diffenbaugh was surprised to see how quickly the new, potentially destructive heat regimes are likely to emerge, given that the study was based on a relatively moderate forecast of greenhouse gas emissions in the twenty-first century. "The fact that we're already seeing these changes in historical weather observations, and that they match climate model simulations so closely, increases our confidence that our projections of permanent escalations in seasonal temperatures within the next few decades are well founded," Diffenbaugh said.[182] Yet industry recently funded the libertarian Heartland Institute to post on billboards language comparing those believing in climate change to the Unabomber. This fortunately brought condemnation from all sides of the political spectrum.[183]

Thomas Friedman, author of *Hot, Flat, and Crowded* argues that we badly need a price signal through mechanisms such as a carbon tax, gasoline tax, or a cap and trade system to encourage change in behavior regarding energy use and climate impact and to spur development of cleaner sources of energy. But this will be very difficult in a "no new tax" political environment.

Global Footprint Network (GFN) is an alliance of scientists that calculates how many Earths we need to sustain our current growth rates. GFN measures how much land and water area we need to produce the resources we consume and absorb our waste, using prevailing technology. On the whole, says GFN, we are currently growing at a rate that is using up the Earth's resources far faster than they can be sustainably replenished, so we are eating into the future.[184] That does not bode well for our grandchildren. All politicians like to claim they are for family values; shouldn't environmental sustainability be one of those important family values issues?

I had to update my writings on this topic after reading an absolutely fascinating new book recently, *Alone in the Universe: Why our Planet is Unique*, by John Gribbin. You don't have to agree with his conclusions to be blown away by his systematic discussion of the origins of the universe, the Milky Way galaxy, our solar system, and the earth. He builds on the very latest scientific understandings to lay out why our planet is in a nearly unique position in our galaxy, making it improbable that there are many, if any, other planets containing advanced life in the Milky Way. Gribbin says in his book: "It seems likely that Earth-like planets are rare. But even if other earths were common, my view is that while life itself may be common, the kind of intelligent, technological civilization that has emerged on Earth may be unique, at least in our Milky Way Galaxy…Whether or not you see the hand of God in any of this, it would mean that we are the most technologically advanced civilization in the Universe, and the only witnesses with an understanding of the origin and nature of the Universe itself."[185]

Science tells us that the Big Bang happened approximately 13.7 billion years ago, but it was not until 4.5 billion years ago that our sun and solar system formed from a collapsing cloud of gas and dust. The first signs of fossil life were found in the ice of Greenland and date back about 3.6 billion years ago. As Darwin says in the *Origin of Species*, "Probably all the organic beings which have ever lived on this earth have descended from some one primordial form, into which life was first breathed." Gribbin says that "the 'primordial cell' was a heat-loving bacterium that may have come to life near an underwater volcanic vent." This may all be very disconcerting to religious fundamentalists, but my religion is not threatened by scientific knowledge. Just as Copernicus and Galileo were threatened by the religious authorities of the time, the church has been able to largely reconcile with science. The Catholic Church, which threatened Galileo with death, now accepts the fossil record, although it may differ over the pace and mechanisms of evolution. So where does that leave us within our faith communities? In his book, *God Species: Saving the Planet in the Age of Humans*, environmental activist Mark Lynas writes "Nature no longer runs the earth. We do. It is our choice what happens from here." Author Mark Brand (publisher of the Whole Earth catalog) is quoted as saying: "We are as gods and have to get good at it."

My own view is that God has given us dominion over this precious creation of Earth. We are possibly uniquely placed in the universe, the only ones to understand that there is a universe and that we have been given a beautiful garden within it, which we can either continue to destroy, or we can be good stewards of the garden God has given us and try to manage and protect it for generations to come. Our population is now 7 billion people on earth, and the ultimate sustainable capacity may be no more than 12 billion people. The world is growing at the rate of a billion additional people every twelve years, so at current growth rates we would reach 12 billion by 2072, well within our grandchildren's lifetimes. The ability to feed, provide clean water, provide health services, and prevent massive violence and genocide within this global population is testing our limits now and will only get worse. With the growth in population and increased resource consumption and pollution, environmental sustainability is at risk. Climate changes are already resulting in altered weather patterns, which will cause global impacts on agricultural production, rising sea levels that could inundate many island societies and devastate countries such as Bangladesh, and increased weather volatility (e.g., severe storms, flooding, droughts, etc. that we have witnessed in recent years). All of these events often cause mass devastation. Also, many of earth's species are disappearing at an alarming rate. On top of this, we live in a dangerous world; The proliferation of nuclear weapons is capable of destroying life as we know it.

Given this context, it is profoundly sad to me to hear the current political debate in which many candidates are proudly antiscience. We don't have to agree what portion of increased carbon dioxide emissions are coming from man's action to be concerned about what the changes means for our grandchildren. Can't we all agree that God would want us to be good stewards of what we have been given? We of all Abrahamic faiths should reflect on Genesis 1:26–28. Jason Chatraw wrote on the online environmental discussion site, SustainLane, about this passage from Genesis:

> Just as many defenders of the environment quote (it) with passion as do those who think all this green talk is just a fad and we should do whatever we want to do with the earth. The word on which everything hangs is "dominion", taken from the Hebrew verb 'radah'. People who think the Bible gives them

license to treat the earth however they want walk on some theologically tenuous ground in claiming that dominion means they can do whatever they want to it. While dominion implies a hierarchy that places humans in charge, it does not implicitly mean humans are to abuse the earth with no regard for the future....Writers all throughout the Bible mention time and again how much God cares for His creation. If this is the case, why would God give us a license to abuse it into oblivion?[186]

Since the current political debate has degenerated to a pathetic point that is largely not relevant to such profound global challenges, can't we within the broad faith communities lead a rational debate about the stewardship of planet Earth? After all, God has given us dominion over it, so shouldn't we at least have some serious discussion about what it means to be good stewards of the beautiful garden in which he has placed us? I am afraid our grandchildren will judge us very harshly if we don't soon take notice of what we are doing to their inheritance, the earth. It could become virtually unsustainable within their lifetimes; is this the legacy we want to leave them?

Social Justice

According to Wikipedia, social justice generally refers to the idea of creating an egalitarian society or institution that is based on the principles of equality and solidarity, that understands and values human rights, and that recognizes the dignity of every human being. The term and modern concept of "social justice" was coined by the Jesuit Luigi Taparelli in 1840, based on the teachings of St. Thomas Aquinas. [187] All the great biblical prophets down through Jesus spoke forcefully about social justice, expressing concern for the meek at the hands of the mighty. For example, Timothy Keller in *Generous Justice* discusses Micah's summary of how God wants us to live: do justice and love mercy. He says the word for justice in this verse is the Hebrew word *mishpat*. Keller says that in its various forms this word occurs more than two hundred times in the Hebrew Old Testament. Its most basic meaning is to treat people equitably. He further comments that after looking at all the places the word occurs in the Old Testament, several types of persons continually come up; those being widows, orphans, immigrants, and the poor. These four groups had little or no social power in these ancient societies. Today this group would likely be expanded to include the refugee, the migrant worker, the homeless, and the elderly. The *mishpat*, or justness of a society, according to the Bible, is evaluated by how it treats these vulnerable groups.[188]

Dr. Cynthia Moe-Lobeda (wife of former assistant pastor at Luther Place, Ron Moe-Lobeda) is the author of a book entitled *Public Church: For the Life of the World*. In the book she does an excellent job of pulling together and summarizing Martin Luther's writings on our need to do social justice. Luther says that the call to serve all people and to strive for justice and peace are understood as expressions of the call "to love neighbor as self." Luther says we live this out in three ways: service to neighbor, disclosing and theologically denouncing oppression or exploitation, and finding ways of living that counter prevailing cultural norms when those norms exploit the vulnerable or defy God in some way. In the New Testament, the great sin is to be deaf to the cry of the poor whether that cry springs from emotional, material, or spiritual need. Although we cannot help but partake to some degree in social injustice because we live in this world, we must constantly reach out in concrete and practical ways to those in need.

Contemporary political rhetoric is challenging the traditional concepts of social justice. For instance, Glenn Beck and some of his following in the Tea Party (who claim to be advancing Christian values) are concerned about the country moving toward socialism, citing legislative passage of measures such as health care or extensions of unemployment insurance as examples. Beck further attacks churches that promote social justice and suggests their interpretations are a perversion of the gospels. Beck went on to state that those promoting social justice have the same philosophy as the Nazis and communists and that the phrase is a code word for both. The Rev. Canon Peg Chemberlin, president of the National Council of Churches of Christ USA, objected to Beck's comments. "I hesitated to respond," she said, "because it seemed like such a ridiculous statement. But this is really an attack…a misunderstanding, at least, of what the Bible says. Justice is a concept throughout the scriptures. It's one that should be and must be organized around any congregation." "It's very disturbing," she added. "He's speaking on behalf of his political views and trying to take out of the biblical text the things that are going to oppose his political views."[189] Other recent criticisms of social justice include Bill O'Reilly writing in the New York Post that "compassion is fine within reason but there is a limit. The Lord helps those who help themselves and the government should do the same…we can't afford to endlessly support the millions of Americans who lack personal responsibility and a strong work ethic."[190] Commentator David Limbaugh (Rush Limbaugh's brother) said on Townhall.com, "So called 'social justice' Christians…are in thrall to supposedly morally superior socialist systems that yield nothing but misery, poverty, tyranny, and subjugation."[191] Could he be referring to more socialist, and predominantly Lutheran, countries like Norway and Finland, whose people report to be among the happiest in the world? Such rhetoric is often more political than religious, but when it distorts biblical concepts of compassion and justice, we need to be prepared to respond.

My church, Luther Place, stands proudly as one of those churches that has social justice in its mission, and it takes that commitment seriously (e.g. establishing N Street Village for homeless women). But, unfortunately, the voices of the mainline churches have for the most part been silent in the face of these recent challenges regarding the biblical concepts of social justice. If we are to be advocates for social justice, it is important for us to further study and reflect on our Judeo-Christian heritage and the implications in the twenty-first century.

In regards to the biblical basis for social justice, perhaps Jesus' reciting of the eight Beatitudes during the Sermon on the Mount (Matthew 5:3–12) provides the most profound articulation of the societal justice God intends for his kingdom. He said blessed are:

- the poor in spirit: for theirs is the kingdom of heaven.
- they that mourn: for they shall be comforted.
- the meek: for they shall inherit the earth.

- they which do hunger and thirst after righteousness: for they shall be filled.
- the merciful: for they shall obtain mercy.
- the pure in heart: for they shall see God.
- the peacemakers: for they shall be called the children of God.
- they which are persecuted for righteousness' sake: for theirs is the kingdom of heaven.

Some have suggested similarities between the role of the Ten Commandments in the Old Testament and that of the Beatitudes in the New Testament; that is, "as God gave the Ten Commandments to Moses, and then the rest of the law is unfolded from them, so Jesus gave the Beatitudes to his followers, and then the rest of the moral implications of the new covenant are unfolded."[192] The message of justice, compassion, and peace are so clear in the Beatitudes that it is difficult to see how so many Christians fail to heed it. Maybe the Beatitudes are just too difficult to deal with, so believers find ways to dance around them. Richard Rohr, in his book *Falling Upward: A Spirituality for the Two Halves of Life*, raises the interesting question of why Christians do not seek to put a stone monument with the eight Beatitudes on the courthouse walls as they try to do with the Ten Commandments? I think we may know the answer.

John Wheaton says in his writing "A Biblical View of Social Justice" that "God has a special interest in the welfare of those at the lowest end of the social ladder: widows, orphans, legal aliens, and others who are oppressed or disadvantaged in society (Jeremiah 7:5-7)."[193] In his book *The Prophet and His Message*, Michael Williams cites numerous passages in which the prophets exhort God's people to give special care to the weaker members of society, the four "withouts": (1) the poor, (2) the orphan, (3) the widow, and (4) the sojourner. The prophets repeatedly indict Israel for failing to carry out social justice within the covenant community. The prophets also remind Israel that they themselves were redeemed from slavery in Egypt; to oppress other members of the community in the land to which they had been delivered would demonstrate callousness to human need and the worst kind of ingratitude for the redemption that God had provided. Jewish theologian Abraham Joshua Heschel says in his book *The Prophets*: "The prophet is an iconoclast challenging the apparently holy, revered, and awesome. Beliefs cherished as certainties, institution endowed with supreme sanctity, he exposes as scandalous pretensions...Our standards are modest; our sense of injustice tolerable, timid; our moral indignation impermanent; yet human violence is...permanent. To us life is often serene, in prophet's eye the world reels in confusion. The prophet makes no concession to man's capacity." The prophet can be relentless in the face of injustice. In many cases, this gets them in trouble with the power structures of the day.

Williams characterizes Jesus as the ultimate prophet who perfectly represents God; he continually articulated the prophetic message of compassion for the "least of these." Marcus Borg describes Jesus' inclusive ministry as "including women, untouchables, the poor, the maimed, the marginalized, as well as some people of stature who found his vision attractive." Jesus challenged the social order of the day with a radically alternative vision that was upsetting to both the religious authorities (Sadducees and Pharisees) and the Roman government. Theologian Walter Brueggemann, in *Interpretation and Obedience*, writes about Jesus' radical ministry of "welcoming the stranger," that is, the outcast in society. Jesus challenged the social arrangements of the day, including the church purity laws of the religious hierarchy; he infuriated the powerful, particularly by sharing a meal with those viewed as unclean.[194] In the banquet parable from Luke 14:19–23 (King James Version); Jesus said:

> A certain man made a great supper, and bade many: And sent his servant at supper time to say to them that were bidden, Come ; for all things are now ready. And they all with one consent began to make excuses. The first said unto him, I have bought a piece of ground, and I must needs go and see it: I pray thee have me excused. And another said, I have bought five yoke of oxen, and I go to prove them: I pray thee have me excused. And another said, I have married a wife, and therefore I cannot come. So that servant came and showed his

lord these things. Then the master of the house being angry said to his servant, Go out quickly into the streets and lanes of the city, and bring in hither the poor, and the maimed, and the halt, and the blind. And the servant said, Lord, it is done as thou hast commanded, and yet there is room. And the lord said unto the servant, Go out into the highways and hedges, and compel them to come in, that my house may be filled.

This example of Jesus' inclusive ministry shows the radical hospitality of welcoming the stranger. This is exactly what my church, Luther Place, did in welcoming the homeless to eat and sleep in our sanctuary starting in the cold winter of 1976. This was an act of welcoming the stranger that no other church in D.C. was willing to follow. It was too threatening to church hierarchies and members to have these "unclean" or "undeserving" people eating and sleeping in our pristine sanctuaries; that space was reserved for the deserving and privileged who came to use it on Sunday morning.

So what we witness in contemporary society and politics is not the first time that Jesus' radical social justice message found resistance from prominent forces in society. In Jesus' case, opponents were so angered that they had him nailed to a cross. In contemporary times, the critics attack policies of helping the needy as socialism and challenge those churches that preach social justice as perverting the gospels. But the crucifixions also go on when the church stands with the oppressed! If you need to be reminded of this reality, simply watch the film *Romero* about the "crucifixion" of Archbishop Oscar Romero in El Salvador as I recently did on the thirty-second anniversary of his death.

A final point to be made regards personal versus societal responsibility for social justice. As important as individual compassion and charity is, our Judeo-Christian heritage also suggests there is a societal (governmental) role in social justice. As Jim Wallis of the Sojourners stated in a recent article:

The biblical prophets, in their condemnations of injustice to the poor, frequently follow those statements by requiring the king (the government) to act justly (a requirement that applied both to the kings of Israel and to foreign potentates). Jeremiah, speaking of King Josiah, wrote, "He defended the cause of the poor and needy, and so all went well" (22:16). Amos instructs the courts (the government) to "Hate evil, love good; maintain justice in the courts" (5:15). Clearly the prophets hold kings, rulers, judges, and employers accountable to the demands of justice. Individuals, families, and congregations are needed to minister to the "least of these," but the Bible says that kings, rulers, judges, employers, and governments also are held biblically accountable to the requirements of justice.

Author and columnist Paul Krugman comments about a Tea Party–sponsored presidential campaign event where the commentator asked candidate Ron Paul whether we would just let a sick uninsured person die, and audience members yelled, "yeah!" Krugman observes that compassion seems to be out of fashion today, at least among the GOP's base. This group of people seems hostile to the kind of society we have, where the government tries to help ordinary Americans in need through such programs as Social Security, unemployment insurance, Medicare, and Medicaid.[195]

This is very obvious in the current Republican primary political debate. Newt Gingrich's rhetoric is no surprise; just before Christmas 2011, he was quoted in Iowa as saying: "This is the most important election since 1860, because there's such a dramatic difference between the best food-stamp President in history and the best paycheck candidate." Not so surprising from Gingrich even at Christmas, but Mitt Romney, the so-called moderate among the Republican field, sounds a similar theme. Romney describes the 2012 election as a battle between the partisans of entitlement and the partisans of opportunity. He goes on to say:

> Will the United States be an Entitlement Society or an Opportunity Society? In an Entitlement Society, government provides every citizen the same or similar rewards, regardless of education, effort and willingness to innovate, pioneer or

take risk. In an Opportunity Society, free people living under a limited government choose whether or not to pursue education, engage in hard work, and pursue the passion of their ideas and dreams. If they succeed, they merit the rewards they are able to enjoy.[196]

I presume that according to Romney, if people get left behind, as in today's economy, that's tough luck for them! Romney's comment exploits public distrust of programs that explicitly serve the poor, the programs that are on the chopping block in most of the Republican candidates' budget proposals. These include programs such as Medicaid, the Children's Health Insurance Program, earned-income tax credits, cash payments to eligible individuals or households such as Supplemental Security Income for the elderly or disabled poor, unemployment insurance, food stamps, school meals, low-income housing, child care, and programs for abused and neglected children.[197] Santorum would go even further; he would cut $5 trillion from the budget over five years. Everything other than entitlement programs and defense would be cut 10 percent from their 2008 rates and would be frozen. Entitlement programs would eventually be cut too. While Santorum's Catholic faith compels him to believe that the poor should be helped, he believes that the government is not responsible for caring for "the least among us" because the aid should come from the people. Sure people contribute to charity but mostly to their church for largely internal programs; I wonder how many people and churches will take in the homeless, the disabled, the unemployed, the abused children, and so forth when government funding is cut.

So, as the Religious Right's, so-called family values voters, favor candidates who are advocating radical reductions in programs for the neediest people, whom Jesus would have ministered to, Progressives of all faiths need to provide an alternative voice. As Newt Gingrich said during his campaign, "the 2012 election may be the most important since 1860." The 1860 election of course, was during the period that the question of slavery was being widely debated, fueled by the likes of Harriet Beecher Stowe in Uncle Tom's Cabin. She was the daughter of the famous Congregationalist minister Lyman Beecher. The Beechers expected all their children to shape their world: all seven sons became ministers, but Harriet became the most influential of the siblings through her writings about slavery. So, that leaves us to ponder where we will find those progressive voices of our time; we surely need them.

War and Religion

Desmond Tutu says in his book, *God is not a Christian*: "We are supposed to proclaim the God of love, but we have been guilty as Christians of sowing hatred and suspicion; we commend the one whom we call the Prince of Peace, and yet as Christians we have fought more wars than we care to remember." James Carroll in his book, *Constantine's Sword*, describes the sad history of religious persecution and war after Christianity became a state religion under Constantine. It includes accounts from the persecution of fellow Christians who didn't subscribe to the preferred religious doctrines of the time, to the pogroms against the Jews, to the Crusades and the many religious wars of Europe in the sixteenth and seventeenth centuries, and the list goes on.

Below are a few quotes from multiple sources about our fascination with war:

From James Hillman's book *A Terrible Love of War*:

- "In the beginning was, not the Word, but War."
- "Could the state of war become normal were it not in tune with something in the human soul."
- "Hypocrisy in America is not a sin but a necessity and a way of life. It makes possible armories of mass destruction side by side with the proliferation of churches, cults, and charities. Hypocrisy holds the nation together so that it can preach, and practice what it does not preach."[198]

Chris Hedges, in his book *War is a Force that Gives Us Meaning*, says "War is a God, as the ancient Greeks and Romans knew, and its worship demands human sacrifice. We urge young men to war, making the slaughter they are asked to carry out a rite of passage. And this rite has changed little over the centuries, centuries in which there has almost continuously been a war raging somewhere on the planet. The historian Will Durant calculated that there have only been twenty-nine years in all of human history during which a war was not underway somewhere." He goes on to say "The cost of war is often measured in the physical destruction but probably worse is the psychological and spiritual toll. This cost takes generations to heal…In the beginning, war looks and feels like love. But unlike love, it gives nothing in return but an ever-deepening dependence, like all narcotics, on the road to self-destruction."[199] We sing and pray "God Bless America" as we triumphantly send our boys off to war. But as is so well communicated in *All Quiet on the Western Front*, war is hell, there is no glory, and it is certainly not something we should ask the Prince of Peace to bless.

In war, both sides are typically praying to the same God for victory. Lincoln said about the Civil War: "Both sides read the same Bible, and pray to the same God; and each invokes His aid against the other.… The prayers of both could not be answered; that of neither has been answered fully."[200]

Christians developed the so-called Just War Theory in the thirteenth century, but it has gradually evolved into a more universal theory of justification for war. Although St. Augustine commented on the morality of war from the Christian perspective, the most systematic statement was developed by Saint Thomas Aquinas in the thirteenth century. In the *Summa Theologicae*, Aquinas presents the general outline of what becomes the traditional just war theory. Aquinas's thoughts became the model for later scholars and legalists to expand and to gradually universalize beyond Christendom. The principles of justification for war are commonly held to be: having just cause, being a last resort, being declared by a proper authority, possessing right intention, having a reasonable chance of success, and the end being proportional to the means used.[201] But all too often the faithful are helping to lead the rush to war.

In his book *God and Empire,* John Dominic Crossan says the faithful must choose "between the violent God of human normalcy and the nonviolent God of divine radicality, between peace through violence and peace through justice...The normalcy of civilization's violence is not the inevitability of humanity's destiny."[202] The prophet Isaiah's visionary message in the Old Testament still is the ideal we should strive for. Isaiah's vision is of a time when God reigns and brings peace to all nations;"He shall judge between the nations, and shall arbitrate for many people; they shall beat their swords into plowshares, and their spears into pruning hooks; nation shall not lift up sword against nation, neither shall they learn war anymore." Jesus, of course, is the prime biblical example of nonviolent resistance for justice, as he and his followers demonstrated time and again against the Roman empire and the religious power structure of the day. Gandhi once wrote that "Jesus was the most active resister known perhaps to history. This was nonviolence par excellence."[203] In the twentieth century, Gandhi, Day, King, and others have given us contemporary examples of the nonviolent path to justice.[204] The nonviolent revolutions in Eastern Europe that brought down the Berlin Wall and the fall of the Soviet Union and the recent, largely nonviolent revolution in Egypt demonstrate that nonviolent resistance is not just an idealist's dream.

John Kelsay, in an article entitled "The Return of the Religious War" discusses the role of religion in wars of the twentieth century. He says "Perhaps as none before it, the 20th century began on a theme of hope for increased cooperation and peaceful initiatives between adherents of the world's religions. On the century's eve, in fact, the 1893 Parliament of World Religions stood as one of the great expressions of such hope, as representatives of various religious traditions championed a world civilization with shared religious values at its core".[205] But it wasn't long until the religious community was again on the war path. Gary Wills, in his book *Head and Heart,* says "War generally heightens religiosity and in America it tends to unite the generations. He further says "That during the Great War (World War I) all churches but the pacifist ones—Quakers and Mormons—swung into line. Some preachers equated fighting with spreading the Gospel." Wills relates that a Baptist minister in California said: "I look upon the enlistment of an American soldier as I do on the departure of a missionary for Burma."[206] The results were devastating. A new book by Adam Hochschild entitled *To End All Wars: A Story of the Loyalty and Rebellion,* 1914–1918 poignantly describes the tragedy of War World I and places a significant blame for World War II on the outcome of World War I. The casualties of World War I were overwhelming. Hochschild says that about a third of German young men who entered the war at the outbreak were killed over the next four and a half years, and it was an even higher ratio for French young men. He goes on to suggest that Germany's defeat and the vindictiveness of the Allies in the peace settlement that followed contributed to the rise of Nazism and the coming of World War II. He also contends that World War I helped lead to the Russian revolution and the eventual takeover by a communist regime that sowed death and terror in peacetime on a scale that surpassed many wars.[207]

After the devastation of World War I (with over 10 million dead), the so called Social Gospel movement was convinced that the evils of war were so great that most would agree that there was a better way to resolve disputes among peoples. This led to the somewhat idealistic Kellogg-Briand pact of 1928 (or Pact of Paris). Led by the United States and France, fifteen countries signed the pact agreeing that "settlement of all conflicts, no matter of what origin or nature that might arise among them should be sought only by pacific means and that war was to be renounced as an instrument of national policy."[208] Despite the Social Gospel movement's success, including the Pact of Paris in 1928, it drew powerful critics who discounted it as being unrealistic. The alarming growth of totalitarian regimes in Europe by 1930 fueled such criticism. Among the staunchest critic in the United States was Reinhold Niebuhr (1892–1971), the noted intellectual and liberal Protestant theologian who claimed that the idealism of the Social Gospel writers, while admirable, failed the test of political realism. For Niebuhr, religion provided a way of thinking about political life that balanced moral and religious ideals against political realities. He asserted that religious faith points not to the abolition of war, but to a hope or ideal that human beings may eventually live in a peaceable kingdom on Earth. Thus religion sets the attainment of peace as an ideal for which people ought to hope and work, but, Niebuhr argued, in particular cases religious values can support war as a tragic, though justifiable means of policy as laid out in the Just War Theory discussed earlier.[209] So, by 1933, when National Socialism and Stalinism were brutally using military force to achieve their aims, the necessity of war as a last resort to resist a growing evil was being advocated by Niebuhr and others.

Unfortunately, during my lifetime, we have had at least two wars supported by many in the religious community that almost certainly didn't meet the test of the Just War Theory: the Vietnam War and Second Gulf War (Iraq). In neither case was war justified as a last resort. Both saw presidents lying and abusing power to justify war expansion, one a Democrat, Lyndon Johnson, and the other a Republican, George W. Bush. Perhaps most disturbing are the lies and abuse of power to justify U.S. intervention in Iraq to rid the country of Sadaam Hussein and his supposed weapons of mass destruction. It is now clear that there were no weapons of mass destruction in Iraq, and there was no link to al-Qaeda terrorists in Iraq. But these were two of the main justifications for the war. It's clear now through several revealing books about the Bush administration that there were so-called neocon zealots like Deputy Secretary of Defense Wolfowitz who were intent on going to Iraq from the first days of the administration. Despite the warnings of Colin Powell about such a misguided adventure, former Vice President Cheney and former President Bush supported the neocon zealots. This shows how dangerous zealots can be in power; intelligence information was misused or fabricated, links to terrorism were fabricated, and those with different views, such as Colin Powell, were scorned. We as a society should always be very suspicious of a rush to war and the rationale for it. It is now clear that in two major wars in our lifetime, Vietnam and Iraq, the reasons for war were misguided and evidence fabricated, and many lives were lost as a result. I like what Republican presidential candidate Ron Paul says in his book *Liberty Defined: 50 Essential Issues That Affect Our Freedom* about those who champion this rush to war: "Chicken-hawks are individuals who dodged the draft when their numbers came up but who later became champions of senseless and undeclared wars when they were influencing foreign policy," Paul writes in his chapter on conscription. "Former Vice President Cheney is the best example of this disgraceful behavior."[210]

Todd Purdum, in a recent *Vanity Fair* article, discusses President Eisenhower's (who was a five-star general) warnings about the military industrial complex and quotes from similar warnings from George Keenan (Cold War architect and eminent scholar). We unfortunately did not heed their warnings, and Purdum concludes that there is little reason to imagine that the trend toward militarization can be reversed in our current age of fear. Purdum goes on to highlight the split in America among the military and civilian classes. The military seems to draw disproportionately from smaller towns and areas of limited economic opportunity, including the inner cities. Meanwhile, the rest of us can go on with our lives largely unaffected and loathe to criticize the deal.[211]

The other disturbing element of the Second Iraq War was the link to religious fundamentalism under George W. Bush's presidency. He told evangelicals that "I believe God wants me to be president." He told *Washington Post* reporter Bob Woodward that he consulted with a higher father (than his own father George H.W. Bush) in deciding to go to war in Iraq. He also used the term "crusade" in one of his war speeches, which served to confirm Muslim fears of the Christians coming on another "crusade" to liberate Baghdad, as they still recall from a millennium earlier. Fundamentalist and evangelical Christians were among the most avid supporters of Bush's war, further underpinning the notion that this was a holy "crusade." How in God's name could Christians be avid supporters of this war that met few if any of the tests of a just war according to Christian doctrine?

The other main rationale for going into Iraq was the attempt to export freedom and democracy to the Middle East countries. The Bush neocons claimed that the Iraq citizens would shower us with flowers and sweets when we liberated them, yet many came to hate us as occupiers. We killed many of their citizens, the so-called collateral damage of war; we abused their prisoners, many who were held with no charges, we bungled the aftermath of war with too few troops to stem violence, inept planning for reconstruction and nation building, and so forth. Sadly, the follies of the British empire in Iraq and other parts of the Middle East during and after World War I illustrate so tragically how we fail to learn from history.

The final bill for U.S. military involvement in Iraq, Afghanistan, and Pakistan could be as high as $4.4 trillion, according to a comprehensive new report "Costs of War," issued on June 28, 2011. It says that in the ten last years, "the federal government has already spent between $2.3 trillion and $2.7 trillion on these wars," say the authors of the study by Brown University's Watson Institute for International Studies. The war dead exceed 6000 but tragically, the number of suicides of veterans far exceeds the number actually killed in combat. More than 6500 veterans commit suicide each year. New disability claims continue to pour into the VA, with 550,000 through last fall. The report puts the number of civilian deaths to date at approximately 137,000, and the total number of deaths attributable to military conflict in these countries, in uniform or out of uniform, at around 225,000. The study also suggests that the number of war refugees and displaced persons now number around 7.8 million.[212]

It is ironic and pathetic that many hard-line conservatives were out in force recently to criticize the Obama administration for the handling of the Libya engagement and for prematurely (in their mind) ending our involvement in the Iraq War. These were many of the same pundits who supported the rush to war in Iraq nine years ago, claiming that the Iraqis would "shower us with flowers." They further postulated that the war would be a short engagement and that it could easily be paid for by oil revenues in Iraq. Given the successful-nine month liberation of Libya juxtaposed against the tragic nine-year war in Iraq, you would think these critics would be too embarrassed to raise their voices in protest; unfortunately, there is no humility in this group.

Early in 2012, Republican presidential candidates (except Ron Paul) were clamoring for war again in the Middle East, this time in Iran. Author Chris Hedges says in reaction:"The longer we cling to the doomed doctrine of permanent war the more we give credibility to the extremists who need, indeed yearn for, an enemy that speaks in the same crude slogans of nationalist cant and violence that they do." Columnist Fareed Zakaria, on CNN, warned that it is easy to start a war but it's very difficult to predict how it will go and where it might end. He suggests we need to ask some hard questions before we start launching the missiles.[213]

Religious progressives need to be much more active and vocal in challenging the rush to war before other options are exhausted, as should have happened in the recent rush to war in Iraq with trumped up claims of weapons of mass destruction in the highest levels of our government. We must also use our soft power (e.g., diplomacy, sanctions) much more effectively before considering the use of hard power, for example, military action. As Joseph Nye suggests in his book *Soft Power:* "America's success will depend upon our developing a deeper understanding of the role of soft power and developing a better balance of hard and soft power in our foreign policy."[214] He calls that balanced approach "smart power." In the case of Iraq, waiting for UN inspectors to report on weapons of mass destruction was seen as unnecessary interference to the Bush administration's rush to implement its new preemptive military strike policy. In a gratuitous last minute sop to the UN, the Bush administration sent Colin Powell to the UN Security Council to make the case for war in Iraq. As it turned out, Colin Powell's remarkable career was tainted by this disaster, as most of the claims made in the presentation turned out to be false. Former top aide to Colin Powell, Colonel Lawrence Wilkerson says his involvement in the former secretary of state's presentation to the United Nations on Iraq's weapons of mass destruction was "the lowest point" in his life.[215] Fareed Zakaria, *Time* columnist, recently discussed the merits of the much more successful Libyan operation where we took the time to pursue options, engage our allies including the Arab world, get UN authorization, and limit the scope to support of an indigenous rebel coalition which would be responsible for post Gadaffi leadership. He suggests this is much more the model for any future interventions.[216]

I include one final thought in this topic offered by a Lutheran pastor, Tim Jahn. He wrote this piece not long after 9/11 and it's a message we should remember at times when religion turns nationalistic, for example, singing God Bless America while our boys are rushed to war (e.g. Iraq). Jahn's offering in part:

God bless America
United we stand
But don't just bless my country
bless the whole land
God Bless Asia
and Africa, too
and if you've been suffering
may God bless you
God bless the homeless
of every creed
whether it's shelter
or a country you need
God Bless the nations
ravaged by war
when no one remembers
what it's all for[217]

5

Thoughts about the Future of the Progressive Movement in Religion and Society

Progressives and the Current Political Environment

So what does this all mean in our twenty-first century society? Columnist Bob Herbert recently commented that the politicians and the media behave as if the poor don't exist. Government data shows that nearly 44 million people were living in poverty in 2009, yet the political leaders seem to be worrying disproportionately about the millionaires and billionaires (e.g., tax cuts for the wealthy and corporations); I guess it's not surprising the number of billionaires who are underwriting the presidential candidate's campaigns. Mitt Romney generated a large controversy when he recently said in an interview on CNN that he doesn't worry about the very poor because they have a safety net. The problem is that Romney's own budget proposal calls for tax cuts and increased defense spending, which implies drastic cuts in domestic discretionary spending to meet the spending reduction targets he has proposed if he became president; so there goes the safety net. Someone else would apparently have to worry about the poor.

Seldom do federal budget decisions have such profound choices for the future direction of America. Decisions made in 2013 budget processes could have huge implications for the future, particularly for our growing senior population and the lower-income population. For example, the House-adopted budget for 2013, spearheaded by Representative Paul Ryan of Wisconsin, would cut Medicare and transfer cost risk to seniors. Medicaid would be given to the states through block grants, thus leaving decisions to the states about who would be dropped from the program, given that the block grants won't keep up with the projected costs. Ryan's deficit reduction plan relies on deep cuts to discretionary spending programs, which tend to support our country's more vulnerable while the better-off are protected. Tax cuts for the wealthy are preserved in the Ryan plan. The tax rate on corporations will be dropped from 35 percent to 25 percent, and defense spending is preserved. Ryan was quoted at the American Enterprise Institute by several sources as saying just after his 2012 budget release that we are at the tipping point in two regards "first, long-term economic decline as the number of makers diminishes and the number of takers grows...and second, gradual moral-political decline as dependency and passivity weaken the nation's character." So it's survival of the fittest under the Ryan plan; so much for Biblical concepts of social justice. Yet the Religious Right applauds these guys. I don't get it. I urge the Religious Right to spend more time getting grounded in the basic message of the Gospels before they enter the political discourse in such anti-Gospel ways. They only need to read the story of the Good Samaritan, which asks: Who is my neighbor? Rev. Dr. Sharon E. Watkins, General Minister and President of the Disciples of Christ comments on this text saying: "When Jesus said, "Love your neighbor as yourself," he didn't just mean exchanging cups of sugar with the family next door. In the story of the Good Samaritan, Jesus showed that being a neighbor means reaching out to anyone, anywhere, in their need. A federal budget that slices away at funds for hungry children and their families, that abandons senior citizens, that reduces life-sustaining foreign aid, is a budget that goes against the teachings of Jesus. America can do better! The Good Samaritan saw a need, reached out to meet the need, and then enlisted the aid of others to help. Through a compassionate federal budget, we can do the same – and be a stronger nation for it!"[218]

Recognizing that increased tax revenues will have to be part of any fair budget deal, Frank Wolf, a Republican congressman from northern Virginia, takes on his own party over its antitax position. He supports closing tax loopholes for big corporations and elimination of other questionable tax exemptions for special interests. David Brooks, Republican commentator, also regularly takes on his own party, particularly the Tea Party segment, who he says do not accept compromise nor the legitimacy of scientific or economic expertise.[219] Despite warnings from the nation's financial leaders last year that not raising the debt ceiling could have calamitous impacts on the financial health of the nation, Republican Congressional leaders held the very financial viability of our country hostage to try to get the president to bow to their demands. The irony is that the Republicans' own budget plan required the debt ceiling to be raised; so their objections to raising the ceiling are disingenuous. We now see what this disastrous approach has yielded: among other results, Standard and Poor's downgraded U.S. debt because of the political morass in Washington over the debt ceiling. This political hostage taking by Tea Party representatives was one of the most irresponsible political acts in our country's history. It seems to be all about their extreme views, no matter that the country sinks into financial crisis. These recent Congressional actions continue policies of recent decades which have increasingly tilted the playing field toward the wealthy. Congress has cut tax rates on high incomes repeatedly and has relaxed the tax treatment of capital gains and other investment income for the wealthy, while labor policies have made it harder for unions to organize workers. Congressional deregulation of financial markets allowed banks and other financial institutions to create financial instruments that tend to enrich wealthy managers and investors while exposing homeowners and pensioners to greater risks.[220]

Many, on the other hand, have criticized President Obama for not fully embracing his own bipartisan fiscal commission plan, which was coauthored by Democrat Erskine Bowles and former Republican senator Alan Simpson. The president did, however, present an alternative budget vision in both 2012 and 2013 that increases taxes on the wealthy and closes certain questionable tax expenditures and reduces military and other spending for total savings of about $4 trillion over ten years. It cuts spending equally from domestic discretionary and defense programs. It also raised taxes on well-to-do Americans in order to both raise revenue and offset reduced tax rates for corporations. But he had no takers on Capitol Hill from either party. Meanwhile, many liberals have criticized the president for not taking more leadership, including taking a stronger stand against Tea Party extremism. He can also be criticized for not more fully embracing his own Simpson-Bowles Commission deficit cutting plan.

It is too early to tell if the Occupy Movement will evolve into a significant force to address some of these inequality issues. Its website describes it as "a leaderless resistance movement with people of many colors, genders and political persuasions. The one thing we all have in common is that We Are The 99% that will no longer tolerate the greed and corruption of the 1%. We are using the revolutionary Arab Spring tactic to achieve our ends and encourage the use of nonviolence to maximize the safety of all participants."[221] The Tea Party and other conservatives have definitely noted the challenge from the left and are on the attack, denigrating the participants and trying to tie any of their lawbreaking and radical views directly to the Democratic Party.[222] But interestingly, columnist David Ignatius sees some similarities between the Tea Party and Occupy Movements. Both have raged against financial elites who led us into a ruinous recession and then were bailed out by Washington elites who are viewed as being in bed with special interests. The Occupy Movement initially focused more on the Wall Street financial elite, and the Tea Party more on the Washington elite, but a case can be made that they are both being driven by similar economic forces in our society.[223] The Occupy Movement may be turning the corner into a more focused and sustained political force; it has brought in legal expertise and has gotten active in monitoring and commenting on proposed financial regulation of Wall Street. So we see the beginnings of transition from street protest to political action intent on changing the rules for the future operation of the financial system.

Interestingly, *Time* magazine identified "the Protestor" as the Person of the Year for 2011; it all started when a poor fruit vendor in

Tunisia set himself ablaze in protest against the repressive political system and the protests against dictatorial political regimes quickly spread to Egypt, Libya, Yemen, Bahrain, Syria, and even Russia. The Occupy Movement has more of a focus on economic disparity but was likely emboldened by the protests around the world.

Given the high stakes, it is important for religious organizations to make their voices heard on these important economic and social issues. An interreligious group led by Sojourners has adopted a pledge called the Circle of Protection, which in part reads: "Budgets are moral documents, and how we reduce future deficits are historic and defining moral choices. As Christian leaders, we urge Congress and the administration to give moral priority to programs that protect the life and dignity of poor and vulnerable people in these difficult times, our broken economy, and our wounded world. It is the vocation and obligation of the church to speak and act on behalf of those Jesus called 'the least of these.' This is our calling, and we will strive to be faithful in carrying out this mission." Others are strongly urged to sign the pledge at: http://www.circleofprotection.us/.

One of the challenges going forward is that of corporate money and influence overwhelming individual speech in the political arena. The freedom of speech of individual citizens as opposed to those of corporations took a major setback in a 2010 Supreme Court ruling on a narrow 5-4 decision by the conservative block of the court. The decision in *Citizens United v. Federal Election Commission* overruled two precedents: *Austin v. Michigan Chamber of Commerce*, a 1990 decision that upheld restrictions on corporate spending to support or oppose political candidates, and *McConnell v. Federal Election Commission*, a 2003 decision that upheld the part of the Bipartisan Campaign Reform Act of 2002 that restricted campaign spending by corporations and unions. The 2002 law, the Bipartisan Campaign Reform Act (McCain-Feingold), banned the broadcast, cable, or satellite transmission of "electioneering communications" paid for by corporations or labor unions from their general funds in the thirty days before a presidential primary and in the sixty days before the general elections. Joined by the other three members of the court's liberal wing, Justice John Paul Stevens said the majority had committed a grave error in treating corporate speech the same as that of human beings. President Obama called it "a major victory for big oil, Wall Street banks, health insurance companies and the other powerful interests that marshal their power every day in Washington to drown out the voices of everyday Americans."[224] This has raised alarm in the Progressive community. Fred Worthheimer, president of Democracy 21, said: "This is the most radical and destructive campaign-finance decision in the history of the Supreme Court." And Bob Edgar, president of Common Cause, said: "Thursday was a bad day for democracy." Former Justice John Paul Stevens wrote in dissent, "The court's opinion is thus a rejection of the common sense of the American people, who have recognized a need to prevent corporations from undermining self government since the founding, and who have fought against the distinctive corrupting potential of corporate electioneering since the days of Theodore Roosevelt." Justice Stevens further said that corporations are not themselves members of "We the People" by whom and for whom our Constitution was established. [225]

As a student of the Constitution and the supporting *Federalist Papers*, I note that Federal Paper No. 52 says that Congress should be dependent upon the "People alone," but our Congress seems to be increasingly dependent upon big funders, particularly corporations. Less than 1 percent of Americans give more than two hundred dollars in political campaigns, so it's obvious where politicians go for their money: to the 1 percent that the Occupy Wall Street movement is targeting. And certainly that money does not come without strings attached. So this is hardly a Congress dependent upon the people alone as envisioned in the Constitution.[226] And, who imagined that a presidential candidacy (Gingrich) might be kept alive largely through the generosity of a Las Vegas gambling magnate with important financial interests in China? Presidential candidate Mitt Romney, in a revealing off-the-cuff remark, said recently at the Iowa State Fair while trying to defend his opposition to ending corporate tax subsidies: "Corporations are people, my friend." I do not believe that corporations are equivalent to people; rather, they are global, market-driven entities who lobby with huge contributions to candidates who support their interests, and Romney is a big recipient of their campaign contributions.

Religious Scholars Provide Perspectives on the need for Progressive Transformation in Religion and Society

For this section, I start with Hans Küng, noted Catholic theologian, who was stripped of his license to teach within the Catholic Church for challenging papal infallibility in the 1960s. He subsequently carried on teaching as a tenured professor of ecumenical theology at the University of Tübingen until his retirement in 1996. Küng has championed the position that the scope of ecumenism is far wider than the Christian denominations and that the ecumenical calling of the Church should embrace the whole earth, including other faiths and the so-called secular world. He gave a lecture in 1991 titled "No Peace Among Nations until Peace Among the Religions," which helped set the stage for the project called Weltethos (Global Ethic). The project was an attempt at describing what the world's religions have in common (rather than what separates them) and at drawing up a minimal code of rules of behavior all religions could potentially accept. This resulted in "Towards a Global Ethic: An Initial Declaration," drafted by Dr. Küng in cooperation with staff and trustees and experts from the Council for a Parliament of the World's Religions. Drawing on many of the world's religious and spiritual traditions, the declaration identifies four essential affirmations as shared principles essential to a global ethic.

1. Commitment to a culture of nonviolence and respect for life
2. Commitment to a culture of solidarity and a just economic order
3. Commitment to a culture of tolerance and a life of truthfulness
4. Commitment to a culture of equal rights and partnership between men and women

This declaration was signed at the Parliament of the World's Religions gathering in 1993 by more than two hundred leaders from over forty different faith traditions and spiritual communities. Since 1993, it has been signed by thousands more leaders and individuals around the world. As such, it established a common ground for people of faith to agree and to cooperate for the good of all.[227] [228] I couldn't think of a better starting point for our look forward at the transformation that is needed in religion and society.

There is increasing recognition of a transformation going on in religion, says Harvey Cox in his recent book, *The Future of Faith*. He says that religious people are increasingly more interested in spiritual disciplines than in doctrines. The result is a universal trend away from hierarchical, patriarchal, and institutional religion. As these changes gain momentum, they evoke an almost point-for point fundamentalist reaction. Fundamentalism, Cox argues, is on graphic display around the globe because it is dying. Cox says this recent move away from dogmatic religion is best explained against the backdrop of three distinct periods of church history:

1. The Age of Faith: for the first three centuries of Christianity, the early church was more concerned with following Jesus' teachings than enforcing what to believe.

2. The Age of Belief: from the fourth to twentieth century, when the church focused on orthodoxy and doctrine.

3. The Age of the Spirit, a trend that began fifty years ago and is increasingly directing the church of tomorrow whereby Christians are ignoring dogma and breaking down barriers between different religions—spirituality is replacing formal religion.

In one of his examples about the Age of Belief, he cites the The Great Schism—the great divide between Western and Eastern Christianity that split the church in 1054. The issue that led to this was a theological question concerning internal relationships within the godhead. More specifically, does the Holy Spirit proceed from the Father and the Son, which was the position of the Western church, or from the Father only, which was the position of the Eastern church? This disagreement leads one to say, how on earth could we possibly know about the internal relations of the godhead? Isn't it finally time to put this silly schism behind us and focus on what is really important, our faith in action?

Dietrich Bonheoffer, similar to Cox, made the distinction between faith and institutional religion. In his prison letters, "Bonheoffer... mused about the emergence of a 'religionless Christianity,' where God would be unclouded from metaphysical constructs of the previous 1900 years...Bonheoffer had a critical view of the phenomenon of religion and asserted that revelation abolished religion (which he called the 'garment' of faith). Having witnessed the complete failure of the German Protestant church as an institution in the face of Nazism, he saw this challenge as an opportunity of renewal for Christianity."[229] Further, Bonheoffer says in regard to justice: "We are not to simply bandage the wounds of victims beneath the wheels of injustice, we are to drive a spoke into the wheel itself."[230]

James Carroll, in his new book *Jerusalem, Jerusalem,* also discusses some of the disenchantment with rigid orthodoxies of organized religion because of its historic intolerance and association with violence; for Christianity, the persecution of other faiths came particularly after Constantine made it the official religion of the Roman Empire. It is not a pretty history, as Carroll describes it in his earlier book *Constantine's Sword.* As we look forward, he says we will have to distinguish between good and bad religion. He lists five characteristics of good religion, including:

1. Celebrating life, not death: good religion shuns apocalyptic assumptions about a punishing god and earthly annihilation; it is about compassion and love, not punishment.

2. Recognizing in God's Oneness a principle of unity among all God's creatures. Oneness assumes differences and respect for those differences; good religion is inclusive, not exclusive.

3. Concerned with revelation, not salvation. Carroll says: "The threat of hell with its assumption of a monstrous God, goes

hand in glove with apocalyptic religion"; this again is counter to the loving God of good religion.

4. Not being coercive. Good religion is never connected to force.

5. It may increasingly have a spiritual and secular character (organized religion is often viewed as tradition bound and historically enmeshed in intolerance and violence). Good religion involves continuing renewal and reformation

In regard to his Catholic Church, James Carroll says in his book *Practicing Catholic:* "Never has the world needed a rational, energized, and fully reformed Catholic Church more, yet never has the Catholic Church's need for reform been more manifest. From the sexual neurosis that abets a multitude of preventable deaths from AIDS, to the ongoing scandal of a hierarchy that refuses to attend to the deeper sources of abuse of children by Catholic priests, to the anti female bigotry enshrined in the all-male priesthood, the Catholic Church is doing serious damage." Yet, he says: "The Catholic people have already changed...Catholics came to understand that they; themselves—not the [hierarchy] are the church," and that, "To be Catholic today is to be in the act of leaving behind the narrow denominationalism of the now finished Reformation." [231]

Jim Wallis, in his book *The Great Awakening* agrees with Carroll when he says "Some people believe the alternative to bad religion is secularism, but that's wrong. The answer to bad religion is better religion—prophetic rather than partisan, broad and deep instead of narrow, and based on values as opposed to ideology. In America (and in most of the developing world) religion is here to stay. The question is not whether faith and spiritual values will be applied to politics, but how?" [232] He believes that faith can enter public life on behalf of social justice in ways that are respectful of democracy, pluralism, and diversity.

Marcus Borg, a prominent Jesus scholar, also reflects on recent trends in organized religion in an interview discussing his book *The Heart of Christianity.* He says: "Broadly speaking, there are two different visions of Christianity in North America today. The earlier vision is the product of the last few hundred years, especially the last 150 years.

This earlier vision of Christianity is literalistic in its understanding of the Bible, absolutist in its understanding of the ethical teachings of the Bible, and exclusivist—meaning Christianity is the only way. That's the vision of Christianity that the majority of us grew up with, whether we are mainline Protestant, Catholic, or conservative Protestant. But that way of seeing Christianity has become unpersuasive to millions of people—who can't be literalists or absolutists or exclusivists. But now there is an emerging vision, an emerging paradigm."

Borg says, "the conflict between these two paradigms can be seen in many different places. In the second half of the 19th Century and early in the 20th Century we saw conflict over evolution. Thirty years ago the conflict was over ordination of women in mainline denominations, and of course today we see the conflict about gays and lesbians in the church. For Protestants, the two visions have everything to do with biblical authority. The earlier vision sees the Bible as a divine product with a divine guarantee to be true. The emerging vision sees the Bible as a human historical product, the product of two ancient communities [Judaism and Christianity]. It tells us what they thought, not what God thinks….I'm persuaded that Christianity, rightly understood, makes sense--and so do Judaism, Islam, Hinduism, and Buddhism; and they make very much the same kind of sense."

As I mentioned earlier in my book, author Gary Wills points out that at the beginning of the twentieth century, the Fundamentalists had their time in the sun, achieving such milestones as Prohibition and the banning of Darwin in the schools. But the Scopes Trial over teaching evolution and the repeal of Prohibition largely brought this era to an end. He suggests that the religious fundamentalists today have gotten so far out of line from mainline religious beliefs regarding human rights, religious freedom, and modern scientific understandings that their influence and membership, particularly among younger evangelicals, is eroding. But mainline denominations have seen a large membership decline as well; I think part of this is due to being turned off by the image of Christianity promulgated widely by the Religious Right and because the version of Christianity they learned growing up (particularly teachings of exclusiveness) ceases to make compelling sense to them today.

In his book, *The Left Hand of God,* Rabbi Lerner talks about the Left Hand and the Right Hand of God. He says, "The Right Hand is the one that portrays God as the powerful avenger, the Force that will overthrow evil…, exterminate enemies, and suppress dissent." This is the war hand that is often played by man in the name of God. Lerner says, "The Left Hand is the force that makes possible a world of nonviolence, peace, and social justice…The human race needs and yearns for the Left Hand of God." This is the Hand of God that says "pursue justice, love one's neighbor as oneself, and never oppress the stranger;;" Rabbi Lerner encourages an interfaith progressive spiritual movement to pursue the Left Hand emphasis of God in order to counter the Religious Right and their unholy marriage with right-wing politicians. He sees a spiritual crisis, a longing for meaning in life, which has attracted seekers to the Religious Right because they had the only visible alternative. Progressives had given up on the institutional church and provided no viable alternative for those searching for more meaning in their lives. There is spiritual yearning that has also manifested itself in alternatives such as the emerging church movement, discussed earlier in this book, which includes many disenchanted with the institutional church or turned off by the exclusionists in the Religious Right.

Matthew Fox, in his book *A New Reformation: Creation Spirituality and the Transformation of Christianity* calls for a new reformation. Like Luther, he presents ninety-five theses, or faith observations, drawn from his years of living and practicing religion and spirituality. He went to Wittenberg and posted them on the church doors where Martin Luther posted his original ninety-five theses, launching the first Christian Reformation. He says: "For me, they represent a return to our origins, a return to the spirit and the teaching of Jesus and his prophetic ancestors, and of the Christ which was a spirit that Jesus' presence and teaching unleashed." [233] Fox emphasizes that we are all called to be prophets and justice seekers.

Desmond Tutu, in his latest book *God Is Not a Christian: And Other Provocations*, says that religion is one of the most important of our formative influences, and in most cases, the religion we take up is a result of the geography of our birth. Unfortunately, through ignorance, we too often assume the religion we were born into is the only true religion. Bishop Tutu says that we must acknowledge and respect believers in other religions for who they are with their conscientiously held beliefs. While we can be proud to hold to our particular beliefs, we must be ready to learn from one another and not claim that we alone possess all truth. After all, Bishop Tutu says, "the Spirit of God existed long before there were Christians, inspiring and nurturing women and men in the ways of holiness, bringing them to fruition, bringing to fruition what was best in all. We do scant justice and honor to our God if we want, for instance, to deny that Mahatma Gandhi was a truly great soul, a holy man who walked closely with God. Our God would be too small if he was not also the God of Gandhi: if God is one, as we believe, then he is the…God of all his people."[234]

In his new book, *Speaking Christian*, Marcus Borg further says that the language of Christianity must also be transformed to become a viable twenty-first century religion. The focus on personal salvation within a heaven-hell framework is particularly problematic. The view that only an in-group of Christians are saved and will go to heaven while the rest of the world is destined for hell is particularly disturbing and not consistent with biblical texts. Borg contends that the use of salvation in the Old Testament had to do with liberation from bondage, as in Exodus, and in the New Testament, salvation is largely about deliverance and transformation from the repression of biblical societies. He contends that in the context of both the Old and New Testaments, salvation was about liberation and peace. Economic injustice and institutional violence was the great cause of human misery in the world of the Bible, and the great prophets, including Jesus, were challenging the powers to restore justice and peace. So Borg contends that salvation is a twofold transformation of us and the world to be more just and peaceful.

N.T. Wright, in his book *Surprised by Hope*, says in regard to salvation: "Mention salvation, and almost all Western Christians assume that you mean going to heaven when you die;…to see the death of the body and the escape of the (soul to heaven) as salvation isn't simply slightly off course,…it is totally and utterly wrong." He contends that 'salvation' in the biblical context is not about going to heaven but being raised to life in God's heaven and new earth. According to Wright, salvation is about being rescued, similar to Borg's description that salvation in the biblical context was about liberation from repression in ancient societies. They suggest that Jesus and the great biblical prophets were challenging the authorities of their time to restore justice and peace here and now; they were not focused on some personalized eternal salvation aspiration.

Even prominent evangelical pastor Rob Bell challenges traditional views of heaven and hell in his new book, *Love Wins: A Book about Heaven, Hell, and the Fate of Every Person Who Ever Lived.* He poses the question: ""Will only a select few people make it to heaven, and will billions and billions of people burn forever in hell?" The idea that there is not a hell and that every person who ever lived could have a place in heaven (whatever that means) has created quite a firestorm within his own evangelical community.[235] As with Wright and Borg, Bell focuses much more on restoring goodness to all in this world (heaven on earth) than on some hereafter where only the select few are redeemed.

Unlike Jesus' radical gospel example, many of today's Christians prefer to take the easy road: to avoid dealing with salvation in the here and now on behalf of all who need to be rescued from repression rather focusing on personal eternal salvation for the benefit of themselves and the other select few of their sect who will be saved. As Wright, Borg, and Bell write, the focus on eternal personal salvation linked with a heaven-hell framework that assumes a select group of Christians will be taken off to heaven while all of God's other children are destined for hell is a disturbing distortion of the biblical message. How did conservative Christianity ever get to this point? It is completely counter to Jesus' ministry of justice to all. Didn't we have a Reformation in which Martin Luther said that God's grace is available to us all, thus freeing us from worrying about seeking personal salvation and allowing us to get on with doing the gospel's justice work to restore the kingdom here and now?

Karen Armstrong, religious historian and author of the book *History of God* and many other thoughtful interreligious publications, says two important things that are particularly relevant to my book. First, she pinpoints fundamentalism in the world's three major monotheistic religions, Judaism, Christianity, and Islam, as the biggest concern facing the faithful, and when extremism turns violent (e.g., jihad in Islam), it is a threat to all of society. Second, she has identified compassion as the most important tenet among the world's major religions, suggesting it is indispensable to the creation of a just economy and a peaceful global community.[236] Building on this belief, she has initiated the Charter for Compassion to promote the principles of the Golden Rule across the religious and global spectrum. The effort is guided by the Council of Sages, a multifaith, multinational group of religious thinkers and leaders.[237]

The Charter affirms the following:

- Compassion is celebrated in all major religious, spiritual, and ethical traditions.
- The Golden Rule is our prime duty and cannot be limited to our own political, religious, or ethnic group.
- Therefore, in our divided world, compassion can build common ground.

So the overriding message from these scholars is that the church is in a historic transformation process, possibly another reformation. Matthew Fox, Phyllis Tickle, and Harvey Cox all suggest we are entering a third great wave of Christianity (maybe a reformation). Cox calls the third wave "The Age of the Spirit," a trend that he says began fifty years ago and is increasingly directing the church of tomorrow in which Christians are ignoring dogma and breaking down barriers between different religions—spirituality is replacing formal religion. Benedictine Sister Joan Chittister says that spirituality is what takes us beyond religious practice to the purpose of religion: the awareness of the sacred in the mundane, the consciousness of God everywhere, in everyone.[238] James Carroll identifies good and bad religion historically and identifies key characteristics of good religion (e.g., nonviolent, not coercive, respecting of all God's creatures) that should come out of the transformation that is going on. Karen Armstrong argues that compassion is the central message of all the world's major religions and has helped draft a Charter for Compassion. Leo Tolstoy said: "True religion is that relationship, in accordance with reason and knowledge, which man establishes with the infinite world around him, and which binds his life to that infinity and guides his actions…and leads to the practical rules of the law: *do to others as you would have them do unto you.*"[239] Hans Küng and the Parliament of the World's Religions in 1993 drafted a declaration intended as a minimal code of ethics for all religions, which is as follows:[240]

1. Commitment to a culture of nonviolence and respect for life
2. Commitment to a culture of solidarity and a just economic order
3. Commitment to a culture of tolerance and a life of truthfulness
4. Commitment to a culture of equal rights and partnership between men and women

So biblical concepts of compassion, tolerance, nonviolence, economic justice, and equal rights are the underpinning of a just society for which the progressive faith communities should be key advocates. With so many justice challenges in our society, some will feel overwhelmed and might ask, where do we start? Mother Theresa says, "Few of us are able to do (in the eyes of the world) 'great things', but all of us can do small things with great love."[241] So pick something you are passionate about and take the first step toward action, even if it is helping just one person; it may truly be transformative in the life of that one person.

From the wisdom of these eminent theologians, scholars, and leaders, I turn to some closing reflections on the path forward for faith and society.

Closing Reflections

In my final reflections on the path forward for the progressive faith/spiritual community (progressive institutional churches, emerging churches/spiritual communities, and the social-justice-oriented secular communities), I draw on the wisdom of other leaders and scholars and then offer my own final thoughts on the progressive way forward.

The Dalai Lama visited N Street Village on October 19, 2007, and I was privileged to greet him and hear him speak. At that event, he stressed compassion for 'the least of these' as he embraced homeless women of N Street (see photo below); he said that compassion and social justice is the common message of all the world's major religions. While lamenting that the twentieth century was a century of bloodshed with two World Wars, the Holocaust, wars in Korea and Vietnam, genocides in Armenia, Cambodia, Bosnia, and Rwanda, among other conflicts around the globe; he remains hopeful for the future. He said: "Despite its faltering start, the twenty-first century could become a great opportunity for dialogue, one in which compassion and the seeds of nonviolence will be able to flourish."

Dalai Lama at N Street Village in 2007

Jim Wallis (of Sojourners), in *God's Politics*, offers a clarion call to make both our religious communities and our governments more accountable to fostering key values of the prophetic religious tradition—that is, make them pro-justice, pro-peace, pro-environment, pro-equality, and pro-family (without making scapegoats of single mothers or gays and lesbians). He suggests that our biblical faith and religious traditions simply do not allow us as a nation to continue to ignore the poor and marginalized, to deny racial justice, to tolerate the ravages of war, or to turn away from the human rights of those made in the image of God. These are the values of love and justice, reconciliation, and community that Jesus taught and that are at the core of what many of us believe, Christian or not. In the tradition of prophets such as Martin Luther King Jr., Dorothy Day, and Desmond Tutu, Wallis inspires us to hold our political leaders and policies accountable by integrating our deepest religious and moral convictions into our nation's public life.

Jean Vanier (founder of the L'Arche movement, communities of radical welcome that include people with disabilities) particularly speaks to those involved with justice efforts for the needy, such as with N Street Village and its ministry to homeless women. In his book *From Brokenness to Community,* Vanier says:

> Communion did not come easily to me. I had to change quite radically. When you have been taught from an early age to be first, to win, and then suddenly you sense that you are being called by Jesus to go down the ladder and to share your life with those who are poor and marginalized, a real struggle breaks out within oneself. But over the years the people I live with have been teaching and healing me. They have been teaching me that behind the need for me to win, there are my own fears and anguish: the fear of being devalued or pushed aside, the fear of opening up my heart and of being vulnerable or of feeling helpless in front of others in pain; there is the pain and brokenness of my own heart. I did not want to admit all the garbage inside me—the elitism that is the sickness of us all. We all want to be on the winning team—that is at the

heart of apartheid and every form of racism. The important thing is to become conscious of those forces in us and to work at being liberated from them. The help of God and the love and support of community gives you the certitude that you are loved just as you are, with all of your wounds. People may come to our communities because they want to serve the poor; but they will only stay once they have discovered that they themselves are the poor. And then they discover something extraordinary: that Jesus came to bring the good news to the poor—not to those who serve the poor. I think we can only truly experience the presence of God and receive the good news, in and through our own poverty. God is present in the poverty and wounds of our hearts. And God is not just present in our capacity to heal but in our need to be healed. God can bring peace and compassion and love through our wounds. Yes, the broken and the oppressed have taught me a great deal and have changed me quite radically—they have taught me what it means to be brothers and sisters in communion and in community. And they have revealed to me the well of tenderness that is hidden in my own heart which can give life to others (pp. 18–25).[242]

Patrick Fermor, in his book *A Time to Keep Silence*, describes visiting four monasteries while looking for a quiet place to write. He was immediately shocked at the "staggering difference" between life inside the monastery and outside in the world. The vows of poverty, chastity, obedience, stability, and community are the exact opposite of the world's infatuation with wealth, promiscuity, independence, freedom, and privacy. His book suggests to me that we all should take time to pull back from the world for reflection, study, and prayer to help put our lives in perspective and renew us for the journey ahead.[243]

Bob Edgar, former congressman and head of Common Cause, in his book *Middle Church: Reclaiming the Moral Values of the Faithful Majority form the Religious Right*, identifies three key issues for a progressive faithful agenda: poverty, peacemaking, and concern for the environment.

Robert Jones, in *Progressive and Religious,* identifies five common characteristics that should underpin a progressive religious orientation. They are an emphasis on social injustice, truth telling, respect for tradition, profound belief in the unity of all humanity, and a new vision in America that emphasizes generosity and interdependence as the foundation of prophetic patriotism.

Rabbi Sidney Schwarz, in his book *Judaism and Justice: The Jewish Passion to Repair the World,* discusses the strong call to justice in the Jewish community and the key Jewish organizations oriented to justice that are attracting the younger generation of Jews. Examples of these are AVODAH: The Jewish Service Corps, which places young college graduates in urban poverty agencies, and the American Jewish World Service, which addresses justice issues around the world.

Ronald Sider, founder of Evangelicals for Social Action and author of *Fixing the Moral Deficit,* says "we have a deficit crisis, a poverty crisis, and a justice crisis and they are all interrelated." He lists key principles from biblical teaching that should guide public policy to fix our deficits in a balanced way. Key aspects are summarized below:

- Radical individualism is not biblical; there is provision for individual freedom, but there is also a communal responsibility.
- The faithful have a special responsibility for the needy and must ensure that proposals to end the deficit crisis protect poorer members of society.
- Economic inequality that harms the poorer in society and places too much power in the hands of a few inevitably leads to greater injustice.
- In biblical teaching, there is a significant and legitimate role for government in caring for the poor, and it is unbiblical to claim otherwise.

So, the emerging view among the theologians reviewed in this book is that religion must be transformed to respond to twenty-first century challenges. Turning inward and backward to an earlier time, as many fundamentalists want to do, will not lead us toward a just and peaceful kingdom. These scholars believe that our biblical faith and religious traditions simply do not allow us as a nation to neglect the poor and marginalized, to deny racial justice, to tolerate the continuing ravages of war, or to turn away from the human rights of those made in the image of God. Douglas Hall, an insightful Canadian professor of theology and author of *The Stewardship of Life in the Kingdom of Death*, says that we are now a global village, and we will all live or die as one planet. Issues such as weapons of mass destruction, AIDS, global warming, terrorism, and poverty are not confined to small parts of the world. These threats to life are widespread, and we cannot afford to view them as not being our problem.

People of God must also recognize that there are many faiths and paths to God, and we must respect and affirm all members of other faiths and not treat them as heathens and try to convert them. We will all have to work together to solve the world's problems. Hall contends that the survival of creation itself is at stake and that our primary faith and societal challenge is to be stewards of the planet and all the people who share it.

My final thoughts on what's needed for the path forward:

1. **We need to rediscover a passion in the progressive faith communities.** As Robert Jones states in his book *Progressive and Religious,* we need the passion exhibited among the great progressive periods in our history:"Colonists fighting for freedom, abolitionists working to end slavery, the struggle to give women vote, the labor movement's organizing for worker rights, the movement to provide a social safety net in the wake of the Great Depression, and the civil rights movement— each of these were driven by passion to overthrow particular injustices." These passionate movements included both secular and religious progressives advocating for social justice, the coalition that we need again today. Otherwise we let the religious and political forces on the far right to dominate the media and move our country backward. Our country was founded on forward-thinking, progressive principles laid out by the likes of Thomas Jefferson and James Madison in

the Declaration of Independence, the Bill of Rights, and the Constitution. Let us honor that tradition.

2. **We need a moral call to action.** The Center for American Progress in its 2010 report says: "The moral call-to-action provided by the progressive religious tradition is desperately needed and warranted at a time when poverty is at record highs and economic inequality reaches levels not seen since the Gilded Age. The core values of human dignity, compassion, cooperation, and solidarity built into these traditions can serve as powerful correctives to the rampant materialism, selfishness, and greed that threaten working- and middle-class families today. Just as religious voices helped spark the great transformations of the previous Progressive and New Deal eras, similarly inspired voices today can take the lead in forming a renewed vision of individual rights, societal duty, and the common good." [244] As mentioned earlier, I was pleased to see the Vatican's Pontifical Council for Justice and Peace issue a strong and thoughtful report in October 2011 on the current financial turmoil in both the United States and Europe. It spoke of ethics over the economy and embraced the logic of the global common good.[245] It supported increased international regulation to curb excesses of the financial markets and to place the common good at the center of international economic activity. The Occupy movement, including Occupy Faith (see photo below), is an indication of the growing grassroots efforts to turn the tide away from inequality in our society and the pernicious influence of big money in our political process. I believe the undue influence of PACs and the idea of individual billionaires largely carrying a presidential political campaign will further spur grassroots efforts to restore balance to political campaigns and our representative democracy.

Ash Wednesday Service with Occupy Faith, led by Luther Place Pastor Karen Brau at McPherson Square, Washington, DC, March 2012

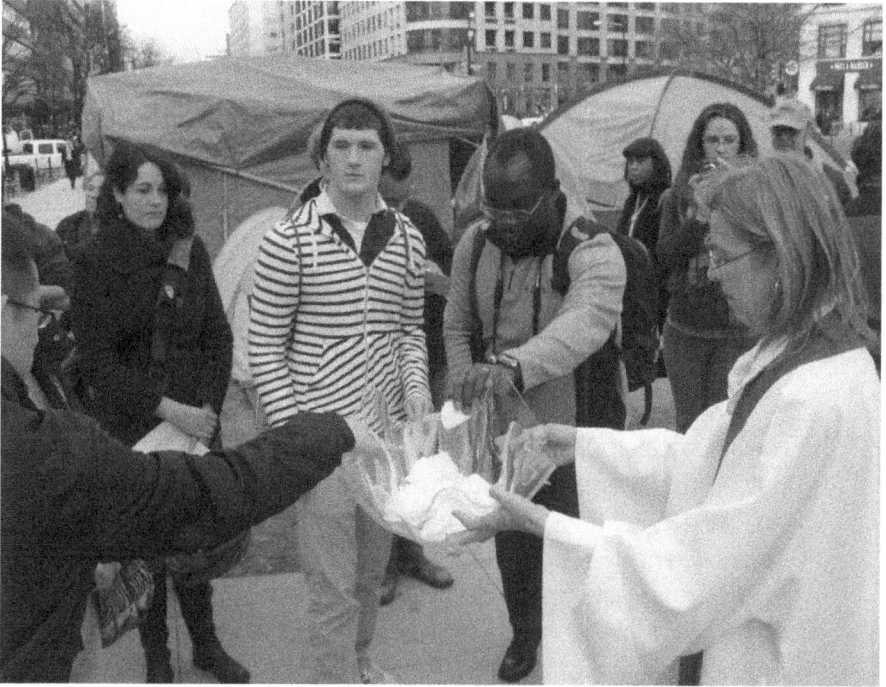

3. **We need to organize for action.** I mentioned earlier the example of the interfaith community, particularly the Washington Interfaith Network (WIN) in Washington, DC, organizing for community action. WIN and other such community organizing efforts follow the tradition of Saul Alinsky, who founded the Industrial Areas Foundation (IAF) during his organizing work in Chicago's working-class neighborhoods in the 1930s and 1940s. Known as the father of community organizing, Alinsky was committed to generating popular participation by those excluded from power. One of the hallmarks of faith-based community organizing is that through it, people actively participate in civic and political

action and don't just write checks to lobbying groups.[246] This is exactly the kind of activity President Obama joined in Chicago after law school; it's also the part of his background that was continually criticized by Sarah Palin and others during the 2008 presidential campaign. Newt Gingrich also recently attacked President Obama as a follower of Saul Alinsky, saying: "the President believes in a kind of Saul Alinsky radicalism which would lead to a secular European socialist model."[247] These reactions all suggest that community organizing is having its impact, and of course, we know that Obama used his community organizing training well in his successful 2008 presidential campaign. This is exactly what concerns the likes of Newt Gingrich as the 2012 presidential campaign progresses.

At the time of his death in 1972, Alinsky was planning to mount a campaign to organize middle-class Americans into a national movement for progressive change; possibly something like the Social Gospel movement of the early twentieth century. The Occupy movement, the latest nationwide effort at organizing for progressive change, did not explicitly follow the Saul Alinsky community organizing tradition, but it is adopting some of the same principles of organizing. Time will tell whether the Occupy movement is a one-shot effort or a sustained movement. In any case, action toward social justice in our communities and the nation will take concerted and sustained organizing across progressive religious, spiritual, and secular sectors. Jim Wallis says faith-inspired activists have always worked alongside those of multiple faiths and those with no religious faith who are motivated by deep moral and ethical commitments. Bridging the gap among multiple religious and secular communities through a service model such as N Street Village has proven successful, but we need to extend such cooperation to community-wide and national political and social advocacy. Sojourners, Faith in Public Life, The Network of Spiritual Progressives, and The New Evangelical

Partnership for the Common Good discussed herein are good examples of what I am advocating.

4. **A call to compassion and justice.** One of the chief tests of our generation is whether we can build a global society that allows people of all religious and political persuasions to live together in peace and mutual respect. As noted earlier, religious historian Karen Armstrong identifies compassion as the most important and common tenet among the world's major religions and the Dalai Lama similarly says that compassion and social justice is the common message of all the world's major religions. If that is so, where are the voices of compassion in the world today? Whether from the public pronouncements of Christian and Islamic fundamentalists, the bishops of Rome, the ultra-orthodox Hasidim in the West Bank, or our political leaders who claim to be representing Christian values, lately one hears few appeals to compassion and justice. Instead, the focus tends to be on matters of sexual conduct or ancient doctrinal disputes, implying that a "correct" view of these issues is the true criterion of faith. Rabbi Abraham Joshua Heschel has said: "Man has often made a god out of dogma… He would rather believe in the dogma than in God…[and] be ready to take other people's lives, if they refuse to share his tenets." Karen Armstrong says: "We can either empathize with those aspects of our traditions, religious or secular, that speak of hatred, exclusion, and suspicion, or work with those that stress the interdependence and equality of all human beings."[248] The choice belongs to each of us.

In closing, I think it appropriate to quote from the devotions of John Donne (1572–1631), "For Whom the Bell Tolls." This meditation inspired Ernest Hemingway's book of the same title and Thomas Merton's book *No Man is an Island*:

No man is an island,
Entire of itself.
Each is a piece of the continent,

A part of the main.
If a clod be washed away by the sea,
Europe(or America) is the less.
As well as if a promontory were.
As well as if a manor of thine own
Or of thine friend's were.
Each man's death diminishes me,
For I am involved in mankind.
Therefore, send not to know
For whom the bell tolls,
It tolls for thee.[249]

Appendix A: Selected Bibliography

Armstrong, Karen. *A History of God*. Alfred A. Knopf, 1993.

Butler Bass, Diana. *Christianity for the Rest of Us*. HarperOne, 2006.

Bell, Rob. *Love Wins: A Book about Heaven, Hell, and the Fate of Every Person Who Ever Lived*. HarperOne, 2011.

Borg, Marcus. *The Heart of Christianity*. HarperCollins, 1989.

———. *Jesus at 2000*. Westview Press, 1998.

———. *Speaking Christian*. HarperOne, 2011.

Brueggemann, Walter. "Welcoming the Stranger." In *Interpretation and Obedience, Chapter 13*. Augsburg Fortress, 1991.

Carroll, James. *Constantine's Sword*. First Mariner Books, 2001.

———. *Jerusalem: Jerusalem*. Houghton Mifflin Harcourt, 2011.

Chittister, Joan. *Welcome to the Wisdom of the World and Its Meaning for You: Universal Spiritual Insights Distilled from Five Religious Traditions*. Wm. D. Erdmans, 2007.

Claibourne, Shane. *Irresistible Revolution*. Zondervan, 2006.

Cox, Harvey. *The Future of Faith*. HarperOne, 2009.

Crossan, John Dominic. *God and Empire*. HarperSanFrancisco, 2007.

Dionne, E. J. *Souled Out: Reclaiming Faith & Politics after the Religious Right*. Princeton University Press, 2008.

Eck, Diana L. *A New Religious America: How a "Christian Country" Has Become the World's Most Religiously Diverse Nation*. HarperOne, 2001.

Edgar, Bob. *Middle Church: Reclaiming the Moral Values of the Faithful Majority from the Religious Right*. Simon and Schuster, 2006.

Fox, Matthew. *A New Reformation: Creation Spirituality and the Trans-formation of Christianity.* Inner Traditions, 2006.

Gibbs, Eddie, and Ryan K. Bolger. *Emerging Churches: Creating Christian Community in Postmodern Cultures.* Grand Rapids: Baker Academic, 2005.

Hall, Douglas. *The Stewardship of Life in the Kingdom of Death.* Library of Christian Stewardship, 1988.

Heschel, Abraham Joshua. *The Prophets.* HarperCollins, 2009.

Jones, Robert. *Progressive and Religious.* Rowman and Littlefield, 2008.

Keller, Timothy. *Generous Justice: How God's Grace Makes Us Just.* Penguin Group (Dutton), 2010.

Küng, Hans. *What I Believe.* Continuum International Publishing, 2009.

Lerner, Michael. *The Left Hand of God* HarperCollins. HarperCollins, 2007.

MacCulloch, Diarmaid. *Christianity: The First Three Thousand Years.* Penguin Books, 2009.

McLaren, Brian. *New Kind of Christianity.* HarperOne, 2010.

Marty, Martin. *When Faiths Collide.* Blackwell Publishing, 2005.

Sider, Ronald. *Fixing the Moral Deficit: A Balanced Way to Balance the Budget.* InterVarsity Press, 2012.

Spong, John Shelby. *Re-Claiming the Bible for a Non-Religious World.* Harper One, 2011.

Thurman, Howard. *Jesus and the Disinherited.* Beacon Press, 1976.

Tickle, Phyllis. *The Great Emergence: How Christianity Is Changing and Why.* Baker Books, 2008.

Tutu, Desmond. *God Is Not A Christian: And Other Provocations.* Harper-Collins, 2011.

Wallis, Jim. *God's Politics.* HarperSanFrancisco, 2005

———. The Great Awakening. Harper Collins Publishers, 2008.

———. God's Politics, HarperSanFrancisco, 2005

Williams, Michael. *The Prophet and his Message.* P&R Publishing, 2003.

Wills, Gary. *Head and Heart.* Penguin Press, 2007.

Wright, N.T. *Surprised by Hope Rethinking Heaven, the Resurrection, and the Mission of the Church.* Harper Collins, 2008.

Wuthnow, Robert. *America and the Challenges of Religious Diversity.* Princeton University Press, 2005.

Notes

1   National Academy of Sciences, http://americasclimatechoices. org/.

2   Rob Bell, *Love Wins: A Book About Heaven, Hell, and the Fate of Every Person Who Ever Lived* (HarperOne, 2011).

3   Marcus Borg, *The Heart of Christianity*, HarperCollins, 1989.

4   KVUE ABC, http://www.kvue.com/news/politics/141567983. html

5   Karen Armstrong, http://www.goodreads.com/author/ quotes/2637.Karen_Armstrong.

6   Wall Street Journal, http://blogs.wsj.com/wealth/2011/03/07/ billionaires-own-as-much-as-the-bottom-half-of-americans//.

7   CNN Money, http://money.cnn.com/2011/09/13/news/econo- my/poverty_rate_income/index.htm

8   http://www.cbpp.org/cms/index.cfm?fa=view&id=3712.

9   Circle of Protection website, http://www.circleofprotection. us//.

10   Christian Science Monitor, http://www.csmonitor.com/Com- mentary/Opinion/2010/0122/Supreme-Court-s-campaign- ruling-a-bad-day-for-democracy.

11   New York Times, http://topics.nytimes.com/top/reference/ timestopics/subjects/c/campaign_finance/index.html.

12   Aljazeera, http://www.aljazeera.com/programmes/peoplean- dpower/2011/10/2011102683719370179.html.

13 Daily Mail, UK, http://www.dailymail.co.uk/news/article-1366451/Illegals-shot-like-hogs-Kansas-State-lawmaker-Virgil-Peck-remains-defiant-immigration-gaffe.html.

14 New York Times, http://www.nytimes.com/2011/11/14/opinion/on-the-rise-in-alabama.html?_r=1&nl=todaysheadlines&emc=tha212.

15 Alabama News, Al.com, http://blog.al.com/live/2012/02/jury_at_bingo_trial_hears_sen.html.

16 Change.org, http://www.change.org/petitions/tell-mecklenburg-county-board-censure-anti-gay-politician-who-called-lgbt-people-sexual-predators.

17 Roll Call, http://atr.rollcall.com/florida-allen-west-claims-communists-in-congress/,

18 MediaMatters for America, http://mediamatters.org/iphone/research/201112120011.

19 Politico, http://www.politico.com/news/stories/0312/73545.html.

20 Right Scoop, http://www.therightscoop.com/cbs-accuses-santorum-of-comparing-obama-to-hitler/.

21 Southern Poverty Law Center, http://www.splcenter.org/blog/2011/10/07/extremists-of-many-stripes-gather-at-values-voter-summit-2011/#more-7976.; Huffington Post, http://www.huffingtonpost.com/2011/10/08/bryan-fischer-mitt-romney-values-voters-summit_n_1001371.html; Washington Post, http://www.washingtonpost.com/todays_paper?dt=2011-10-09&bk=A&pg=1.; NPR, http://www.npr.org/2011/10/07/141162214/a-look-at-the-values-voter-summit.

22 God Discussion, http://www.goddiscussion.com/82020/following-this-weekends-summit-value-voters-group-launches-a-national-bus-tour-to-mobilize-christian-voters; Right Wing Watch, http://www.rightwingwatch.org//.

23 Christian Newx Wire, http://www.christiannewswire.com/news/4907219327.html.

24 Congressional Budget Office, http://www.cbo.gov/ftpdocs/124xx/doc12485/10-25-HouseholdIncome.pdf.

25   Sojourners, http://sojo.net/blogs/2012/03/20/same-budget-problems-new-budget-year.

26   HuffingtonPost,http://www.huffingtonpost.com/2012/04/24/paul-ryan-challenged-by-georgetown-faculty_n_1449437.html

27   Ronald Sider, *Fixing the Moral Deficit*; IVP books, 2012.

28   Bureau of the Census, http://www.census.gov/newsroom/releases/archives/income_wealth/cb11-157.html.

29   Chris Hedges, *Death of the Liberal Class*, Nations Books, 2010

30   *Social Justice in the OECD –How Do the Member States Compare?*, http://www.bertelsmann-stiftung.de/bst/de/media/xcms_bst_dms_34886_34887_2.pdf.

31   The Online Library of Liberty, http://oll.libertyfund.org/?option=com_staticxt&staticfile=show.php%3Ftitle=2286&chapter=218853&layout=html&Itemid=27

32   Time, Tenth Annual History Issue, 2011.

33   Gary Wills, *Head and Heart* (Penguin Press, 2007).

34   Beliefnet, http://www.beliefnet.com/News/Politics/2000/09/I-Believe-In-An-America-Where-The-Separation-Of-Church-And-State-Is-Absolute.aspx.

35   ABC News, http://abcnews.go.com/blogs/politics/2012/02/both-catholic-health-assn-and-planned-parenthood-say-theyre-pleased-with-contraception-rule-announcement//.

36   ELCA, http://www.elca.org/What-We-Believe/Social-Issues/Social-Statements/JTF-Human-Sexuality.aspx

37   The Rise and Fall of the Progressive Republican, Angelo Lopez blog.

38   The Rise and Fall of the Progressive Republican, Angelo Lopez blog.

39   Center for American Progress, http://www.americanprogress.org/issues/2010/10/pdf/progressive_traditions6_execsumm.pdf.

40   Center for American Progress, http://www.americanprogress.org/issues/2010/10/progressive_traditions6.html.

41   Eugene Robinson, *Washington Post* Op-ed, July 19, 2011.

42   Washington Post, http://www.washingtonpost.com/blogs/ blogpost/post/michele-bachmann-signs-pledge-that-says- pornography-should-be-banned-and-homosexuality-is-a- choice/2011/07/08/gIQAnhrf3H_blog.html.

43   Ornstein and Mann, *It's Even Worse Than It Looks: How the American Constitutional System Collided With the New Politics of Extremism,* Basic Books, 2012

44   Paul Krugman, New York Times; Plutocracy, Paralysis, Perplexity; May 3, 2012

45   Politico, http://www.politico.com/news/stories/0212/73337_ Page2.html#ixzz1ni24HWtH.

46   The NewYorker, http://www.newyorker.com/ reporting/2010/10/18/101018fa_fact_wilentz?.

47   Wikipedia, http://en.wikipedia.org/wiki/Cleon_Skousen

48   John Petrie collection of Hayek quotes, http://jpetrie.myweb. uga.edu/hayek.html.

49   Fareed Zakaria, "The Gridlock We Can Fix,," *Washington Post,* July 21, 2011.

50   James Wallis, Sojourners website, http://sojo.net/magazine/2010/11/theology-tea-party.

51   David Campbell, *"Crashing the Tea Party,"* New York Times, August 16, 2011..

52   Pew Forum, http://pewforum.org/Politics-and-Elections/Tea-Party-and-Religion.aspx.

53   BookBrowse, http://www.bookbrowse.com/author_interviews/full/index.cfm/author_number/423/karen-armstrong.

54   John Shelby Spong, *Re-Claiming the Bible for a Non-Religious World* (Harper One, 2011).

55   Gary Wills, *Head and Heart* (Penguin Press, 2007).

56   BookBrowse, http://www.bookbrowse.com/author_interviews/full/index.cfm/author_number/423/karen-armstrong.

57   Gary Wills, *Head and Heart,* Penguin Press, 2007

58   Huffington Post, http://www.huffingtonpost.com/amy-sullivan/sharia-myth-america_b_876965.html.

59   Martin E. Marty, *The Collision of Faiths* (Blackwell Publishing, 2005).

60   Diana Eck, *A New Religious America: How a ""Christian Country""
     Has Become the World's Most Religiously Diverse Nation.*

61   Former Bush administration official David Kuo, *Tempting Faith:
     An Inside Story of Political Seduction, Free Press, 2006*

62   National Journal, http://www.nationaljournal.com/njmaga-
     zine/st_20100501_5904.php.

63   Naomi Cahn and June Carbone are family law professors at
     George Washington University and the University of Missouri
     (Kansas City),); Cahn and Carbone, *Red Families v. Blue Families:
     Legal Polarization and the Creation of Culture* (Oxford Univer-
     sity Press 2010).

64   Washington Post, http://www.washingtonpost.com/opin-
     ions/the-marriage-gap-presents-a-real-cost/2011/12/16/
     gIQAz24DzO_story.html.

65   New York Times, http://www.nytimes.com/2012/02/17/opin-
     ion/krugman-moochers-against-welfare.html?nl=todayshead
     lines&emc=tha212.

66   http://www.washingtonmonthly.com/archives.php.

67   "Women, Money, and Power;," *Time,* March 26, 1012.

68   Daily Kos, Feb. 8, 2012, http://www.dailykos.com/
     story/2012/02/08/1062989/-Religious-Leaders-Support-Presi-
     dent-Obama-on-Contraception-Rule

69   Ballotpedia, http://www.ballotpedia.org/wiki/index.php/
     North_Carolina_Same-Sex_Marriage,_Amendment_1_
     (May_2012); Charlotte Observer, http://www.charlotteob-
     server.com/2012/05/08/3227863/amendment-one-nc-voters-
     approve.html

70   Wikipedia, http://en.wikipedia.org/wiki/List_of_scandals_in-
     volving_evangelical_Christians, http://en.wikipedia.org/wiki/
     Ted_Haggard

71   Southern Poverty Law Center, http://www.splcenter.org/
     blog/2011/10/07/extremists-of-many-stripes-gather-at-
     values-voter-summit-2011/#more-7976., Huffington Post,
     http://www.huffingtonpost.com/2011/10/08/bryan-fischer-
     mitt-romney-values-voters-summit_n_1001371.html., Wash-
     ington Post, http://www.washingtonpost.com/todays_

paper?dt=2011-10-09&bk=A&pg=1., National Public Radio, http://www.npr.org/2011/10/07/141162214/a-look-at-the-values-voter-summit.

72   National Public Radio, http://www.npr.org/2011/10/07/141162214/a-look-at-the-values-voter-summit.

73   Religion Dispatches, http://www.religiondispatches.org/dispatches/joannabrooks/5229/why_romney_won%E2%80%99t_stand_up_to_the_bigotry_of_bryan_fischer_/_/.

74   Southern Poverty Law Center, http://www.splcenter.org/blog/2011/10/07/extremists-of-many-stripes-gather-at-values-voter-summit-2011/#more-7976.; Huffington Post, http://www.huffingtonpost.com/2011/10/08/bryan-fischer-mitt-romney-values-voters-summit_n_1001371.html.; Washington Post, http://www.washingtonpost.com/todays_paper?dt=2011-10-09&bk=A&pg=1.; National Public Radio, http://www.npr.org/2011/10/07/141162214/a-look-at-the-values-voter-summit.

75   http://www.telegraph.co.uk/news/worldnews/us-election/9154650/Rick-Santorum-under-fire-over-ranting-right-wing-pastor.html.

76   *"Moving Beyond the* 'Religious Right,'" *Washington* Post Op-ed, November 11, 2011.

77   Wikipedia, http://en.wikipedia.org/wiki/Evangelicalism.

78   Jerusalem Center for Public Affairs, http://www.jcpa.org/cjc/cjc-heilman-s05.htm.

79   Wikipedia, http://en.wikipedia.org/wiki/Haredi_Judaism.

80   Diana Eck, *A New Religious America: How a "Christian Country" Has Become the World's Most Religiously Diverse Nation.*

81   Robert Wuthnow, *America and the Challenges of Religious Diversity* (Princeton University Press, 2005).

82   Washington Post http://www.washingtonpost.com/todays_paper?dt=2011-10-08&bk=A&pg=4.

83   Huffington Post,http://www.huffingtonpost.com/2012/02/21/mormons-posthumous-baptism-anne-frank_n_1292102.html

84   Bob Edgar, *Middle Church,* (2006).
85   PBS, http://www.pbs.org/wnet/religionandethics/week845/ interview1.html.
86   ht Gerardo Marti, Davidson College, *The Emerging Church Movement and Young Adults,* tp://www.changingsea.net/studies/Marti2.pdf.
87   Gibbs and Bolger, Emerging Churches: Creating Christian Community in Postmodern Society, 2005, (Baker Academic, 2005).
88   Janet I. Tu, ""*Emerging Churches' Drawing Young Flock,*" by Janet I. Tu, *Seattle Times* staff reporter.
89   Sojourners, http://www.sojo.net/index.cfm?action=magazine. article&issue=soj1005&article=is-the-emerging-church-for-whites-only.
90   Minnesota Public Radio, http://minnesota.publicradio.org/display/web/2008/01/30/houseofmercy/.
91   Christianity Today, http://www.christianitytoday.com/ct/2005/september/16.38.html?start=1.
92   New Monasticism Network, http://new-monasticism-network. ning.com/.
93   Interpreter Magazine, http://www.interpretermagazine.org/ interior.asp?ptid=43&mid=14285.
94   American Progress, http://www.americanprogress.org/issues/2009/05/pdf/millennial_generation.pdf.
95   USA Today, http://www.usatoday.com/news/religion/2010-04-27-1Amillfaith27_ST_N.htm.
96   Sojourners, http://www.sojo.net/index.cfm?action=action.home.
97   See the following website to view the Circle of Protection: https://secure3.convio.net/sojo/site/Advocacy?cmd=display&page=UserAction&id=419http://blog.sojo.net/2011/07/21/matthew-25-why-we-went-to-the-white-house/.
98   Network of Spiritual Progressives, http://spiritualprogressives. org/newsite/?page_id=303.
99   New Evangelical Partnership for the Common Good, http:// www.newevangelicalpartnership.org/?q=node/1.
100   Evangelicals for Social Action, http://www.evangelicalsforsocialaction.org/page.aspx?pid=290

101 Interfaith Alliance, http://www.interfaithalliance.org/about.

102 World Union for Progressive Judaism, http://www.wupj.org/About/About.asp.

103 Faith and Politics Institute, http://alabama2011.wordpress.com/2011/03/06/strengthening-politics-with-faith/.

104 United Church of Christ, www.ucc.org

105 Christian community Development Association, http://www.ccda.org/about.

106 Luther Place Memorial Church, http://lutherplace.org/newsite/template/index.cfm.

107 N Street Village, http://www.nstreetvillage.org/.

108 Lutheran Volunteer Corp, http://www.lutheranvolunteercorps.org/.

109 NHI Shelterforce Online, http://www.nhi.org/online/issues/115/Warren.html.

110 Washington Interfaith Network, www.windc-iaf.org

111 Bert Silver, Soviet Jewry talk, August 2011 at B'nai Israel.

112 Wikipedia, http://en.wikipedia.org/wiki/Common_good.

113 Vatican Archive, http://www.vatican.va/archive/hist_councils/ii_vatican_council/documents/vat-ii_cons_19651207_gaudium-et-spes_en.html.

114 BBC, http://www.bbc.co.uk/programmes/b00lb6bt.

115 Washington Post, http://www.washingtonpost.com/opinions/the-vatican-meets-the-wall-street-occupiers/2011/10/26/gIQAGO8EKM_story.html.

116 ZENIT, www.zenit.org

117 Robert Reich, *Aftershock*, Random House, 2010

118 Fareed Zakaria, "Broken Bootstraps," *Washington Post* Op-Ed, November 10, 2011.

119 "U.S. Firms Eager to Add Foreign Jobs," *Wall Street Journal*, November 22, 2011.

120 CBS 60 Minutes, http://www.cbs.com/primetime/60_minutes/video/?pid=56dmxv0KFpwol5sHx0AqvHaXiDQw2jxo.

121 Doug's Views, http://www.dougberger.net/archive/2011/04/60-minutes-carried-big-corp-water-on-tax-rate-story.html.

122 Nicholas Kristof, *New York Times*, July 7, 2011. http://www.ny-times.com/2011/07/07/opinion/07kristof.html?nl=todayshea dlines&emc=tha212.

123 Bloomberg news, http://www.bloomberg.com/news/2012-01-24/carried-interest-debate-gains-momentum.html

124 New York Times, http://www.nytimes.com/2011/08/15/opin-ion/stop-coddling-the-super-rich.html?nl=todaysheadlines& emc=tha212.

125 Slate, http://www.slate.com/articles/news_and_politics/the_ great_divergence/features/2010/the_united_states_of_in-equality/introducing_the_great_divergence.html.

126 Institute for Policy Studies, *America's Bailout Barons*, September 2009

127 Washington Post http://www.washingtonpost.com/ opinions/what-history-teaches-us-about-the-welfare-state/2011/07/01/AGGfhFuH_story.html.

128 Wikipedia, http://en.wikipedia.org/wiki/Financial_Crisis_In-quiry_Commission.

129 Truth Dig, http://www.truthdig.com/report/item/at_last_ some_decency_on_wall_street_20120314//. New York Times, http://www.nytimes.com/2012/03/14/opinion/ why-i-am-leaving-goldman-sachs.html?pagewanted=2&_ r=1&ref=business. Daily Mail, http://www.dailymail.co.uk/ news/article-2115352/Greg-Smith-Goldman-Sachs-sees-2bn-wiped-market-value-trader-attacks-firms-toxic-culture.html.

130 Timothy Geithner, "A Dodd-Frank Retreat Deserves a Veto," *Wall Street Journal*, July 20, 2011.

131 Harold Myerson, "Corporate America's Chokehold on Wages," *Washington Post*, July 20, 2011.

132 Sojourners, http://www.sojo.net/index.cfm?action=media. display_article&mode=P&NewsID=9357.

133 Presidential Prayer Team, http://www.presidentialprayerteam. org/weeklyprayerupdates/Update-110421.html

134 Thomas Geoghegan, "Get Radical: Raise Social Security," *New York Times*, June 19, 2011.

135 Michael Spence, "*The Impact of Globalization and Employment,*" *Foreign Affairs*, July/August 2011

136 New York Times, http://www.nytimes.com/2011/09/17/opinion/blow-for-jobs-its-war.html?_r=2&hp; http://seekingalpha.com/article/293684-middle-class-poverty-continues-to-grow; New York times, http://www.nytimes.com/2011/09/17/opinion/blow-for-jobs-its-war.html?_r=1&nl=todaysheadlines&emc=tha212.

137 Bernard Sanders, "Is Poverty a Death Sentence??", CommonDreams.org, September 14, 2011 by CommonDreams.org.

138 New York Times, http://www.nytimes.com/2011/12/03/opinion/blow-newts-war-on-poor-children.html?_r=1&ref=charlesmblow.

139 CBS News, http://www.cbsnews.com/8301-503544_162-57335118-503544/newt-gingrich-poor-kids-dont-work-unless-its-illegal/

140 Tax Policy Center analysis of Presidential candidates' 9-9-9 tax plan; October 18, 2011.

141 Wikipedia, http://en.wikipedia.org/wiki/Living_wage.

142 Reclaim Democracy, http://reclaimdemocracy.org/articles_2004/costco_employee_benefits_walmart.html.

143 Washington Post, http://www.washingtonpost.com/wp-dyn/content/article/2007/10/19/AR2007101901543.html.

144 *The Authority of Scripture*, a sermon by John W. Wimberly, Jr.; Pastor, Western Presbyterian Church, Washington, DC.

145 Bill Keller, "A Decent Proposal," *New York Times* Magazine, July 3, 2011.

146 Ted Olson, former Bush administration official; www.mainjustice.com

147 New York Post, http://www.nypost.com/p/blogs/capitol/more_good_ideas_on_immigration_reform_FL0MxE57Pqvkj WqiUrNwDN#ixzz1R4EzmuVG.

148 U.S. Conference of Catholic Bishops, http://usccb.org/issues-and-action/human-life-and-dignity/immigration/churchteachingonimmigrationreform.cfm.

149 Wikipedia, http://en.wikipedia.org/wiki/DREAM_Act.

150   Free   Public,   http://www.freerepublic.com/focus/f-news/2811425/posts.
151   IPS Press Service, http://ipsnews.net/news.asp?idnews=40301.
152   CBS   News,   http://www.cbsnews.com/2100-18560_162-3701249.html?pageNum=2&tag=contentMain;contentBody.
153   God   Discussion,   http://www.goddiscussion.com/86172/saudi-leaders-if-we-let-women-drive-there-will-be-no-more-virgins/?utm_source=feedburner&utm_medium=email&utm_campaign=Feed%3A+GodDiscussion+%28God+Discussion%29.
154   Compass, http://compassreview.org/autumn04/4.html.
155   Doctrinal Assessment of the Leadership Conference of Women Religious; April 18, 2012
156   New York Times, http://www.nytimes.com/2012/04/29/opinion/sunday/kristof-we-are-all-nuns.html
157   Brennan Center, http://www.brennancenter.org/content/resource/voting_law_changes_in_2012.
158   Winning   Progressive,   http://www.winningprogressive.org/tag/koch-brothers
159   Smart on Crime, http://www.2009transition.org/criminaljustice/index.php?option=com_content&view=article&id=27&Itemid=23.
160   Centers for Disease control, www.cdc.gov
161   CBS News, http://cnsnews.com/news/article/personhood-effort-still-alive-despite-its-defeat-mississippi
162   *The New Yorker,* June 6, 2011.
163   National Public Radio, http://www.npr.org/templates/story/story.php?storyId=124784784.
164   Matt Miller Online, http://www.mattmilleronline.com/paul-ryan-hasa-point.php.
165   T. R. Reid; *The Healing of America, A Global Quest for Better, Cheaper, and Fairer Health Care;* Penguin Books, 2009
166   New York Times, http://www.nytimes.com/2011/07/14/opinion/14kristof.html?nl=todaysheadlines&emc=tha212.
167   "How Health Care Reform Can Sink or Save America," *Foreign Affairs,* July/August 2011.

168   Mark Ehlers blog, http://ehlersoneverything.blogspot.com/2012/02/matter-of-perspective.html.
169   World Union of Deists, www.deism.com/Einstein
170   Wikipedia, http://en.wikipedia.org/wiki/Relationship_between_religion_and_science.
171   U.S. Courts, http://www.pamd.uscourts.gov/kitzmiller/kitzmiller_342.pdf
172   *National Academies of Science Press, www.nap.edu*
173   World Union of Deists, www.deism.com/Einstein
174   ELCA Campus Ministry, http://www.elca.org/Growing-In-Faith/Ministry/Campus-Ministry/Campus-Ministry-Articles-and-Guides/Faith-and-Science-in-Dialogue.aspx
175   Butler University, http://blue.butler.edu/~mzimmerm/rel_evolution_weekend_2009.htm.
176   Chris Mooney and Sheril Kirshenbaum *Unscientific America, How Scientific Illiteracy Threatens our Future,* BasicBooks, 2010
177   TownHall, http://townhall.com/news/religion/2012/01/09/evolution_pastors_unconvinced_lifeway_survey_shows_but_theyre_split_on_earths_age
178   Wall Street Journal online, http://online.wsj.com/article/SB10001424052970204468004577167003809336394.html
179   Chronicle of Higher Education, http://chronicle.com/article/State-Budget-Cuts-for-Research/130369/
180   Wikipedia, see topic 'Carbon dioxide in earth's atmosphere'
181   National Academy of Sciences, http://americasclimatechoices.org/.
182   Stanford University, http://news.stanford.edu/news/2011/june/permanent-hotter-summers-060611.html.
183   Washington Post, May 4, 2012; article entitled, *Sign linking global-warming believers to Unabomber pulled.*
184   New York times, http://www.nytimes.com/2011/06/08/opinion/08friedman.html?_r=1&ref=thomaslfriedman.
185   John Gribbin, *Alone in the Universe: Why our Planet is Unique,* John Wiley and sons, Inc., 2012

186   Sustain Lane, http://www.sustainlane.com/reviews/q-what-does-the-bible-mean-when-it-says-we-are-to-have-dominion-over-the-earth/LTI7NKHJW1N23RUS4HCLLVRXR98X.

187   Wikipedia, http://en.wikipedia.org/wiki/Social_justice.

188   Timothy Keller, *Generous Justice: How God's Grace Makes Us Just* (Penguin Books, 2010).

189   Peg Chemberlin, National Council of Churches of Christ, http://www.huffingtonpost.com/peg-chemberlin/christians-run-as-fast-as_b_495166.html

190   New York Post, http://www.nypost.com/news/opinion

191   TownHall, http://townhall.com/columnists/davidlimbaugh/page/2011.

192   The Way of the Lord Jesus, http://www.twotlj.org/G-1-26-A.html.

193   Christian Worldview, http://thechristianworldview.com/tcw-blog/archives/741

194   Walter Brueggemann, *Interpretation and Obedience,* (Chapter 13).

195   New York Times, http://www.nytimes.com/2011/09/16/opinion/krugman-free-to-die.html?_r=1&nl=todaysheadlines&emc=tha212.

196   USA Today, 12/19/2011

197   New York Times, http://campaignstops.blogs.nytimes.com/2011/12/25/the-anti-entitlement-strategy/?ref=opinion&nl=todaysheadlines&emc=thab1.

198   James Hillman, *A Terrible Love of War, The* Penguin Press, 2004, New York

199   Chris Hedges, *War is a Force that Gives Us Meaning*, Anchor Books, 2003

200   Abraham Lincoln online, http://showcase.netins.net/web/creative/lincoln/speeches/quotes.htm.

201   Internet Encyclopedia of Philosophy, http://www.iep.utm.edu/justwar//.

202   John Dominic Crossan, *God and Empire, HarperSanFrancisco, 2007*

203   Thomas Merton, *Gandhi on Nonviolence* (New York: New Directions, 1964).

204   *The Sacrament of Civil Disobedience* (Fortkamp Publishers, 1994).

205   Research in Review, http://rinr.fsu.edu/fallwinter99/features/religiouswar.html.

206   Gary Wills, *Head and Heart* (Penguin Press 2007).

207   Adam Hochschild, *To End All Wars: A Story of the Loyalty and Rebellion 1914-1918, Houghton Mifflin Harcourt, 2011*

208   The Free Dictionary, http://encyclopedia2.thefreedictionary.com/Kellogg-Briand+Pact.

209   Research in Review, http://rinr.fsu.edu/fallwinter99/features/religiouswar.html.

210   New York times, http://www.nytimes.com/2011/11/26/opinion/ok-now-ron-paul.html?_r=1&nl=todaysheadlines&emc=tha212.; Transcript of Ron Paul book, http://www.slideshare.net/kynize/liberty-defined-50-essential-issues-that-affect-our-libertys-by-paul-ron

211   Vanity Fair, http://www.vanityfair.com/politics/2012/01/Todd-Purdum-on-National-Security.

212   Costs of War, http://costsofwar.org//.

213   CNN   World,   http://globalpublicsquare.blogs.cnn.com/2011/11/13/zakaria-dont-rush-to-war-with-iran//.

214   Joseph S Nye, Jr.; *Soft Power, The Means to Success in World Politics; Public Affairs, 2004*

215   CNN,   http://articles.cnn.com/2005-08-19/world/powell.un_1_colin-powell-lawrence-wilkerson-wmd-intelligence?_s=PM:WORLD.

216   Fareed Zakari, "How the Lessons of Iraq Paid Off in Libya," *Time*, September 5, 2011.

217   Marina.com/tag/community; May 2, 2011

218   Sojourners,   http://sojo.net/blogs/2012/03/20/same-budget-problems-new-budget-year34.

219   Mother Jones, http://motherjones.com/kevin-drum/2011/07/brooks-republicans-no-longer-normal.

220 Foreign Affairs, http://www.foreignaffairs.com/articles/67046/ robert-c-lieberman/why-the-rich-are-getting-richer.

221 Occupy Wall Street, http://occupywallst.org//.

222 Politico, http://www.politico.com/news/stories/1011/65826. html.

223 Washington Post, http://www.washingtonpost.com/opinions/around-the-world-rage-against-the-elites/2011/10/11/ gIQA0UkykL_story.html.

224 New York Times, http://www.nytimes.com/2010/01/22/us/ politics/22scotus.html.

225 Christian Science Monitor, http://www.csmonitor.com/Commentary/Opinion/2010/0122/Supreme-Court-s-campaign-ruling-a-bad-day-for-democracy.

226 New York Times, http://www.nytimes.com/2011/11/17/opinion/in-campaign-financing-more-money-can-beat-big-money.html?_r=1&nl=todaysheadlines&emc=tha212.

227 http://www.parliamentofreligions.org/_includes/FCKcontent/File/TowardsAGlobalEthic.pdf.

228 Wikipedia, http://en.wikipedia.org/wiki/Towards_a_Global_ Ethic:_An_Initial_Declaration.

229 Wikipedia, http://en.wikipedia.org/wiki/Dietrich_Bonhoeffer.

230 Goodreads, http://www.goodreads.com/author/ quotes/29333.Dietrich_Bonhoeffer.

231 James Carroll, *Practicing Catholic,* Houghton Mifflin Harcourt, 2009, New York

232 Jim Wallis, *The Great Awakening* (HarperCollins, 2008).

233 Yes Magazine, http://www.yesmagazine.org/issues/spiritual-uprising/1326.

234 This talk also comes from a forum in Britain, where Tutu addressed leaders of different faiths during a mission to the city of Birmingham in 1989.

235 Rob Bell, *Love Wins: A Book About Heaven, Hell, and the Fate of Every Person Who Ever Lived,* (Harper One, 2011).

236 Wisdom Commons, http://www.wisdomcommons.org/author/Karen%20Armstrong

237 Charter for Compassion, http://charterforcompassion.org/about

238 Joan Chittister, *Welcome to the Wisdom of the World And Its Meaning for You: Universal Spiritual Insights Distilled from Five Religious Traditions.*

239 Leo Tolstoy, *Confessions.*

240 Charter for Compassion, http://charterforcompassion.org/share/the-charter

241 The Church of the Ascension, *Small Things Matter;* July 24, 2011

242 Jean Vanier, *From Brokenness to Community,* Paulist Press, 1992

243 Patrick Fermor, *A Time to Keep Silence,* with introduction by Karen Armstrong; New York Review Books Classics, 2007

244 Center for American Progress, http://www.americanprogress.org/issues/2010/10/pdf/progressive_traditions6_execsumm.pdf

245 National Housing Institute, http://www.nhi.org/online/issues/115/Warren.html

246 Truthout, http://www.truth-out.org/newt-gingrich-and-real-saul-alinsky/1328364727, May 2012

247 Bill Moyers essay; February 3, 2012; http://billmoyers.com/segment/bill-moyers-essay-the-real-saul-alinsky/

248 Mark Ehlers blog, http://ehlersoneverything.blogspot.com/2012/02/matter-of-perspective.html

249 Wikisource, http://en.wikisource.org/wiki/Meditation_XVII

www.ingramcontent.com/pod-product-compliance
Lightning Source LLC
Chambersburg PA
CBHW060922040426

42445CB00011B/741